Charles Shearer Keyser

Penn's treaty with the Indians

Charles Shearer Keyser

Penn's treaty with the Indians

ISBN/EAN: 9783337057435

Printed in Europe, USA, Canada, Australia, Japan

Cover: Foto ©Thomas Meinert / pixelio.de

More available books at **www.hansebooks.com**

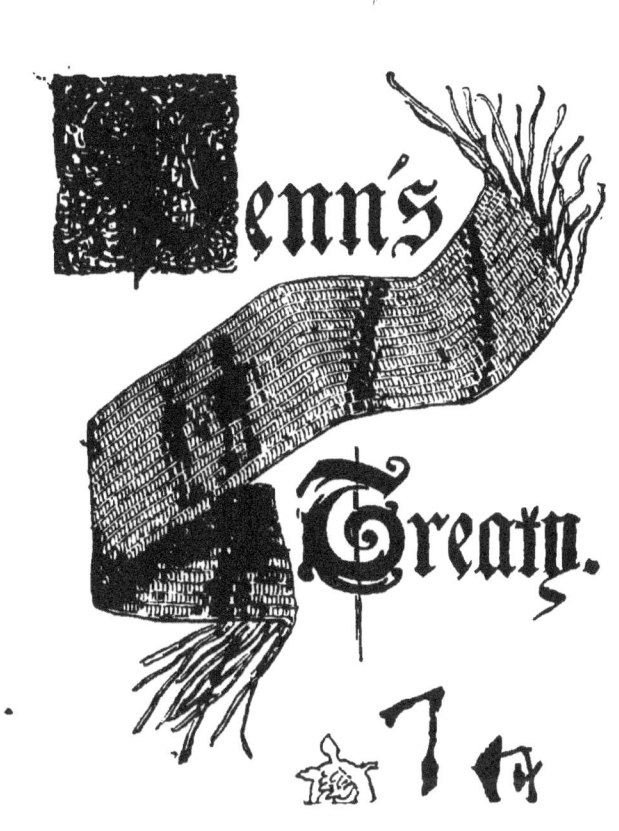

Penn's Treaty.

CHARLES S. KEYSER,
Author of "FAIRMOUNT PARK."

Penn's Treaty

with the

Indians.

CHARLES S. KEYSER.

PHILADELPHIA:
DAVID McKAY,
No. 23 South Ninth Street.
1882.

TO
HORACE J. SMITH,
OF
GEORGE'S HILL
A DESCENDANT OF JAMES LOGAN,
THE
FRIEND AND COMPANION
OF
WILLIAM PENN.

PREFACE.

IN this book is narrated, as our fathers transmitted it to their children, the story of the Treaty, the Founder of our State made with the Aborigines, at Shackamaxon. To its pledges his children and his followers were true; unbrokenly for generations. We preserve its memory, sacred in act and spirit in our generation, "so that his and our posterity will be as a long chain of which he was the first link, and when one link ends another succeeds and then another, being all firmly bound together in one strong chain to endure for ever."

Two Centuries have passed away since it was made, "but these are but a few years and like as yesterday in the life of a nation; nevertheless, following that Great Man's peaceable Councils, this government has now become wealthy and powerful in Great Numbers of People."

PHILADELPHIA, 1882.

CONTENTS.

	PAGE
DEDICATION	v
PREFACE	vii
IN MEMORIAM	ix
PENN'S TREATY	1
THE LINKS IN THE CHAIN OF THE TRADITION	15
THE LAND TITLES	22
THE GREAT TREATY	35
THE TRADITION AMONG THE INDIANS	68
STATEMENTS OF THE WRITERS	70
THE TREATY TREE	88
THE FOUNDER'S WORK AND WORTH	94
POSTFACE	100

ILLUSTRATIONS.

DESIGN, PENN'S TREATY	(to face Title)
WEST'S TREATY	8
TAWARAH'S SIGNATURE	14
THE PORTRAIT IN ARMOR	16
A STRING OF WAMPUM	21
TAMANEN'S SIGNATURE	22
A STRING OF WAMPUM	34
THE WAMPUM BELT	35
THE NATIONAL MUSEUM PORTRAIT	36
LASSE COCK'S SIGNATURE	56
THE TREATY TREE	57
A STRING OF WAMPUM	67
THE WAMPUM BELT	68
THOMAS CLARKSON	82
MALEBONE'S SIGNATURE	85
THE PROPRIETARY ARMS	87
THE PENN MONUMENT	92
AN ELM BRANCH	93
THE PENN ARMS	99

IN MEMORIAM.

"WHEN WE COMMEMORATE THE MANY BENEFITS BESTOWED ON THE INHABITANTS OF THIS COLONY, THE RELIGIOUS AND CIVIL LIBERTIES WE POSSESS, AND TO WHOM THESE VALUABLE PRIVILEDGES ARE OWING, WE SHOULD BE WANTING TO OURSELVES AND THEM WE REPRESENT DID WE NOT DO JUSTICE TO THE MEMORY OF OUR WORTHY ANCESTOR, A MAN OF PRINCIPLES TRULY HUMANE, AN ADVOCATE FOR RELIGION AND LIBERTY."—A. HAMILTON, 1734.

PENN'S TREATY.

THIS memorable treaty[1] was made in the latter part of the month of November, in the year 1682. The place was Shackamaxon[2] on the Delaware River, now a portion of one of the wards of the City of Philadelphia. It was then the site of an Indian village. An Elm Tree stood there, which for its relation to the event was preserved thereafter by the Colonists, and British Soldiers, through the Revolution; it was still standing there until the early part of the present century, when it fell during a heavy storm[3]. Three nations of the

---

[1] "The great Treaty was not for the purchase of lands but confirming what Penn had written, and Markham covenanted, its sublime purpose was the recognition of the equal rights of humanity."—*Bancroft*, Vol. II., p. 383.

[2] "Sakima—the place of Kings; 'Sakima' means a King in the Delaware language—'ing,' is the Indian termination indicating locality, or the place where Chiefs meet, or resort for conferences or treaties."—*H. S. of Pa.*, Vol. III., p. 11, p. 113.

[3] Midnight, March 5–6, 1810. "The Register," March 7, 1810. Merc. Library.

The daughter of the last owner of this tree married a chief of the Cherokee Nation, Lewis Downing, who served during the rebellion in the Union army; they are both (1882) deceased.

A coarse piece of Indian pottery was found embedded in the roots when it was blown down.—*Martin's Chester*, p. 53.

Aborigines had their representatives in the Assemblage, the Lenni Lenape, or Delawares, the Mengwe, or Six Nations, and the Shawanese Nation, which had gone Northward from the South to the Susquehanna; the tribes of the Gawanese and the Conestogas, had also their representatives[1]. Tradition assures us that the Founder was accompanied by members of his Council; also by his Interpreter[2]; by members of his persuasion, and by Dutch and Swedes—the first settlers, drawn there, by their interest, or their curiosity[3]. In the changed condition of the locality by the wharves, and by the streets and houses, its original character, is yet

[1] " Lenni Lenape is synonymous with the Delawares; Mingoes or Mengwe, with the Iroquois, and five and six nations."—*Heckewelder*, p. xxxiv.

The name Iroquois was given by the French.—*La Trobe's Loskiel*, p. 2.

The name Lenni Lenape means original people; "a race of human beings who are the same that they were in the beginning, unchanged and unmixed;" the name has also been defined as " Indians of the same nation."—*Heckewelder*, p. xii.

The Lenni Lenape are never heard to say, " the six nations," and it is a rare thing to hear these people named by them otherwise than Mengwe.—*Ib.*

The Shawnese and Shawanese were the same nation, the Conestogas were Mingoes, the Gawanese was a tribe of one or the other of these nations.

[2] " The Swedes acted as his interpreters, especially Capt. Lasse Cock."—*Acrelius M. H. of Pa.*, Vol. XI., p. 114. " He spelled his name also Lass Cock. His house was near the place."—*Pa. Arch.*, Vol. I., p. 48. The name is a contraction of Lawrence.

" He feared there might be some fault in the Interpreter, being neither Indian nor English."—*Penn to Soc. of Free Traders*, Aug. 6, 1683.

[3] Swedes and Dutch.—*Dixon*, p. 199.

" The first Dutch Colonies settled on the Delaware in 1630; the Swedes arrived in 1631; Friends were settled on the Western side of the river before the City was laid out, at Shackamaxon, where they held meetings; the titles of several Swedes in that neighborhood are as early as 1665-6. Jurian Hartzfelder in March, 1676, took up 350 acres in Campington, Northern Liberties."

readily and certainly, traceable. It was a sloping bank extending down to the sandy margin of the river. The river bordering on one side, and the surrounding forests, forming the enclosure of a wide amphitheatre of green sward, reaching up to, and around the Elm; the Tree was one of the largest of its species, and even then venerable in years[1]. The forest trees which covered the City's site when the Founder landed, and which were described at the time, extended over this locality and far beyond. They were Walnuts, clumps of Chestnuts, stately Oaks, other Elms, Beech trees, Cedars, Cypress and Pines[2], reaching backward toward the Western horizon —the forest walls of this wide amphitheatre; they have long since fallen under the axe and time; the open river yet flows, as it flowed there, centuries agone. The season was November[3]—the Indian Summer; on the

---

[1] At its fall, the circles of annual growth which its bark exhibited, then indicated an age of 283 years.—*M. H. S. of Pa.*, Vol. VI., p. 240. It was twenty-four feet in circumference.—*Ib.*, Vol. I., p. 96.

At the time of the treaty, the ever memorable Elm Tree, was a veteran of the forest, one hundred and fifty years old.—Samuel Breck in *H. S. of Pa.*, Vol. VI., p. 213.

[2] "The trees of most note are the Black Walnut, Cypress, Chestnut, Cedars—the fruit I find in the woods are white and black mulberries, plums—grapes of various sorts—the woods are adorned with lovely flowers."—*Penn to the Soc. of Free Traders.* William Penn, said they, when he treated with them adopted this ancient mode of their ancestors, convened them under a grove of shady trees."—*Heckewelder*, p. 185.

[3] "Near the close of November."—*Janney*, p. 203.

river near the shore lay the Governor's Barge[1], its broad pennant lifting and dipping, only with the motion of the waves. Near the great Elm the Council fire was blazing; its pillar of cloud rising through the hazy slumberous atmosphere, a witness between the heaven and the earth of the unbroken faith pledged there, and to endure. Beneath the wide spreading shadows of the Elm the leaders of the Tribes were gathered; no warlike weapons were in their hands[2]. In front, the old chiefs and their Counsellors; behind them the younger Braves, circle after circle, widening outward towards the West; with them aged matrons, and children[3]. In the assemblage, as was long believed, was Tamanen[4], Sachem of

[1] "His favorite mode of travelling was by water; he kept a Barge furnished with a sail and manned by a cockswain and six oarsmen."—J. F. Fisher in *Mem. of H. S. of Pa.*, Vol. III., p. 11.

"For this barge he always showed much solicitude, he mentions it in his letters to James Logan frequently, and in one says, 'But above all dead things my barge; I hope nobody uses it on any account, and that she is kept in a dry dock, or at least covered from the weather.'"—*Penn and Logan Correspondence.*

"The condition of the roads made travel by boat necessary."—*Ib.*

[2] "Nor would they even permit any war-like weapons to remain within the limits of their council fire, when assembled together about the ordinary business of government."—*Heckewelder.*

[3] "Their order is thus: The King sits in the middle of an half moon, and has his council, the old and wise on each hand. Behind them or at a little distance sit the younger fry in the same figure."—*Penn to the Soc. of the Free Traders*, 1683. Hist. Soc. Lib.

[4] "Tamanend was an ancient Delaware chief, he was in the highest degree endowed with wisdom, virtue, prudence, charity, affability, meekness, hospitality, in short with every good and noble qualification that a human being may possess. He was supposed to have had an intercourse with the great and good Spirit; for he was a stranger to everything that is bad."—*Heckewelder*, p. 300.

the Delawares. The savages, dark to blackness, by their ruder intercourse with the weather, gorgeous with various dyes upon their persons, feathers of the forest birds upon their foreheads, shimmering in the Autumn sun. The Dutch in the well-worn clothes of their voyage, or the more homely leggings and shoes made by the Indians themselves, to which the first landers ultimately came; the Swedes in their Frocks and Trousers, and moccasins of Deer skins, contrasting with the capped and heavy Dutchmen, with their pipes, and imperturbable repose. The immediate followers of the Founder in the quaint costumes of their time—coats reaching to the knees, covered with buttons, most ample vests, trousers slashed at the sides, and tied with strings or ribbons, perukes and low shoes—the one, as the other, except in the more or less expensive material, befitting his circumstances. In the midst the Founder, his hair, parting in many ringlets, over his broad forehead and shoulders; the ruffles of the time, falling over his fair hands, and breast as clear; in his costume distinguished from the others, by his blue silken knit sash, only[1]. Himself, the cause and force of that event, which should survive by his faith and confidence in humanity, to the latest generations. Near him Markham, his trusty

[1] " He was distinguished only by wearing a sky blue sash made of silk net work, and which was of no larger apparent dimensions than an officer's military sash, and much like it except in color."—*Clarkson*, Vol. II., p. 265.
 The sash is now (1813) in the possession of Thomas Kett, Esq., of Seething Hall near Norwich.—*Ib.*, p. 265.

Secretary, in the rich costume of the English Service; Holmes, his Surveyor-General; Symcox, Haigne, Taylor, and Pierson[1]. So they stood together, the passing and the coming race; the race that should perish, and the race that should survive—upon this carpeting of the fallen leaves, whose crimson green and gold arabesques were fading into the sombre dyes of these November days—beneath that Tree whose vast embrace and century growing arms was yielding insensibly as themselves, to inevitable decay: The waning year, the dying leaves, presaging the future of all their forest strength, and painted glories. Yet not here as elsewhere by the deadlier passions of advancing civilization, but for the good faith of the savages, and to the eternal glory of the Founder of Pennsylvania, by the inevitable law of change and dissolution only. Of all these Penn alone survives, in common memory. In stature, tall and athletic; in manner courteous; in disposition most resolute; tender of every person and thing, that had simplicity of truth or honesty for a foundation[2].

He advances toward the Council fire with kindly, courtly dignity; his attendants precede him bearing presents which they lay upon the ground. That venerable Sachem, Taminen, or it may be another as venerable, and distinguished for his wisdom and courage, rises,

---

[1] *Clarkson*, Vol. I., p. 265. *Janney*, p. 203. *Dixon*, p. 109.

[2] "Tender of every person and thing that had simplicity of truth or honesty for a foundation." The testimonial of the Philadelphia Meeting, 16, 1st Mo., 1718-19, following his death.—*Friend's Library*, Vol. V., p. 328.

advances a few paces, puts on his head a chaplet [1], into which is twisted a small horn, the symbol of his authority. By this custom of the Delawares the spot has become sacred, the person of every one there, inviolable. He then devoutly turns his Calumet [2] to the heavens and the earth, seats himself on the ground and smokes a while in silence. The Interpreter announces that he will hear the words of the White Father [3]. Penn addresses them in these sentences, some repeated as

[1] "One of the Sachems who was the chief of them, then put upon his own head a kind of chaplet in which appeared a small horn.—This, as among the primitive Eastern Nations and according to the Scripture language was an emblem of kingly power; and whenever the chief who had a right to wear it, put it on, it was understood that the place was made sacred and the persons of all present inviolable."— *Clarkson*, Vol. II., p. 265.

[2] "The meeting is opened by the head Chief or President who smokes for a short time out of the pipe of Peace after it has been devoutly turned to the Heavens and the Earth. The ceremony is of such importance that no European Governor or Ambassador can make peace with the Indians without it. Afterwards the pipe is handed about among all the Ambassadors and Members of the Council, when each of them takes it up very cautiously and smokes for a short time."—*La Trobe's Loskiel*, P. 1., Ch. X., p. 156.

"The Pipe of Peace (Calumet, fr.) has a large head of red marble three inches deep and six or eight inches wide, but the red color being the color of war, it is daubed over with white clay or chalk. The pipe is made of hard black wood wound with a fine ribbon neatly decorated with white corals by the women. Sometimes ornaments are added made of Porcupine quills with green, yellow and white feathers."—*La Trobe's Loskiel*, P. 1., Ch. X., p. 156.

[3] Miquon was the name which the Lenni Lenape gave to William Penn. The Iroquois called him Onas. Both of these words in their respective languages signify a quill or pen."—*Duponceau, Ann. of Penn's landing*, 1824, note. F. Ins. Library.

"The true signification of William Penn's name belongs to the Welsh or Celtic language from which it is derived. In that tongue the word Penn means head, and metaphorically a leader or chief."—*Hugh's Penn*, p. 90.

The original by Sir Benjamin West, in the National Museum, Philadelphia.

his language long after by the savages themselves, some as they appear in the stories of his life, as his words on the occasion.

"The Great Spirit rules in the Heavens, and the Earth. He knows the innermost thoughts of men. He knows that we have come here with a hearty desire to live with you in peace. We use no hostile weapons against our enemies—good faith and good will towards men are our defences. We believe you will deal kindly and justly by us, as we will deal kindly and justly by you." He then read them the conditions of the league, which were preserved by his successors, and forty years after read to the successors of these representatives of their tribes and nations, article by article.

He then continued: "We will not be to you as brothers—brothers sometimes contend with brothers. We will not be to you as fathers with children—fathers sometimes punish their children. Nor shall our friendship be as the chain that rust may weaken, that the tree may fall upon and sunder. We will be as one heart, one head, one body; that if one suffers, the other suffers; that if anything changes the one, it changes the other [1].

"We will go along the broad pathway of good will to each other together."

They listen to the words in silence as was their custom, they consult among themselves, they deliberate.

[1] *Clarkson*, Vol. I., p. 266, followed by the other biographers.

Taminen orders one of his chiefs to answer; this one rises and advances toward the Founder and salutes him in the King's name. He takes him by the hand[1] and pledges him kindness and good will, that it was the King's mind that these pledges should be accepted and kept by them forever; that the Indians and the Christians shall live in love together as long as the sun gave light in the heavens. He delivers into the Founder's hands that Wampum belt[2] which was thereafter transmitted as an heirloom to his family, and which was given by the last survivor of that family into the keeping of our State Society. One of these belts when given, sealed a single sentence, or the silence of a pledge which should remain sacred forever. This

[1] "Having consulted and resolved their business the King ordered one of them to speak to me. He stood up, came to me and in the name of his King saluted me, then took me by the hand and told me he was ordered by his King to speak to me, and that now it was not he, but the King who spoke, because what he should say was the King's mind."—*Penn to the Soc. of Free Traders*, 1683. H. S. of Pa. Library.

[2] "It is a belt of the largest size, and made with the neatest workmanship, which is generally found in such as are known to have been used in Councils, or in making treaties with the Indians. Its length is twenty-six inches, its breadth is nine inches, and it consists of eighteen strings woven together; it is formed entirely of small beads strung in rows, and made from pieces of clam or muscle shells. These form an entirely white ground: in the centre there is a rude but striking representation, worked in dark violet beads, of two men—the one, somewhat the stouter, wearing a hat; the other, rather thinner, having an uncovered head; they stand erect, with their hands clasped together; there are three bands, also worked in dark violet beads, one at either end, the other about one-third the distance from one end, which may have reference to the parties to the treaty, or to the rivers Delaware, Schuylkill, and Susquehanna.

"It was presented to the Historical Society of Pennsylvania, on the 25th day of May, 1857, by Granville John Penn, a descendant of the Founder. It is framed

done, another speaks to the tribes in the name of all
the Sachamakers and Kings repeating to them, this that
was done; then commanding them by the words of
these Kings that they should live with the Founder and
his people in peace forever—the great Assemblage[1] of
these Kings and braves standing among their women
and children, at each sentence of these pledges, repeated in their language, shouted, and in their way said
Amen[2].

The conditions of the league—the pledges of that
memorable treaty—the links of the enduring chain, that
the falling tree broke not, nor time nor change weakened,
as they were preserved in the archives of our State, and
as they were read forty years after for the last time to

between glass plates and hangs from the ceiling of a fire-proof room built within the
Hall of the Society. The copy was made in exact fac-simile of the original belt.

[1] "They were seen in the woods as far as the eye could carry, so that dismay and
terror had come upon them, had they not confided in the righteousness of their
cause."—*Clarkson*, Vol. I., p. 264.

"Nineteen Indian Nations (tribes)."—*Oldmixon*, London, 1708, p. 171. First
edition *Hist. Soc. Library.*

[2] "Which done another made a speech to the Indians in the name of all the Sacha-
machers or Kings; first to tell what was done: next to charge and command them
to love the Christians and particularly to live in peace with me and the people under my government; that they should never do mine or me any wrong. At every
sentence of which they shouted, and in their way said, Amen."—*Penn to the Society of Free-Traders.* "These ceremonies are always attended with dancing."—
La Trobe's Loskiel, P. 1., p. 155.

"It is said that the Founder, who inherited some portion of his wholesome Dutch
mother's exuberance of spirits, as well as the more stable qualities of her blood,
took part in the dancing on his first reception by the Indians 'and excelled them
all' but unless, as one of the necessities of the assemblage, it would here seem beneath the gravity of the occasion."—See *Watson*, p. 131.

the representatives of these tribes—the Ganawese, the Conestogas, and the nations, of the Delawares and of the Shawanese, were these:

"We will be brethren, my people and your people, as the children of one father.

"All the paths shall be open to the Christian and the Indian. The doors of the Christian shall be open to the Indian, and the wigwam of the Indian, shall be open to the Christian.

"The Christian shall believe no false stories, the Indian shall believe no false stories, they shall first come together as brethren and inquire of each other; when they hear such false stories they shall bury them in the bottomless pit.

"The Christian hearing news that may hurt the Indian, or the Indian hearing news that may hurt the Christian, shall make it known the one to the other, as speedily as possible, as true friends and brethren.

"The Indian shall not harm the Christian, nor his friend; the Christian shall not harm the Indian, nor his friend; but they shall live together as brethren. As there are wicked people in all Nations; if the Indian or the Christian shall harm the one or the other, complaint shall be made by the sufferer, that right may be done; and when right is done, the wrong shall be forgotten, and buried in the bottomless pit.

"The Indian shall help the Christian, and the Christian shall help the Indian, against all evil men, who would molest them[1]."

The words in which the final pledge was given following their custom and in its language were:

"We will transmit this League between us to our children. It shall be made stronger and stronger, and be kept bright and clean without rust or spot, between our children and our children's children, while the creeks and rivers run, and while the sun, moon, and stars endure[2]."

And so this Treaty was made, and has become a part of our first inheritance of freedom; a part of the Christianity of the world. And very truly to the faith pledged there, as no other people; have the Founder's followers proved during the last two centuries since that Treaty's Pledge, in season and out of season, steadfast; wherever the Indian has called out from the suffering of his endless march, the Quakers of the Founder's City have answered the enduring "Yea."

Yet there have not been wanting men even here, where he walked, when on earth, and where the river

[1] Cited by Governor Gordon at the Council at Conestoga, May 26, 1728, *H. S. of Pa.*, Vol. III., p. 2, page 202.

[2] " Great promises passed between us of kindness and good neighborhood, and that the English and Indians must live in love as long as the sun gave light."— *Penn to the Society of Free-Traders*, 1683, Aug. 16.

" At the concluding speech, the Indians generally make use of this expression, that their friendship shall last as long as the sun and moon give light, rise and set; as long as the stars shine in the firmament, and the rivers flow with water."—*La Trobe's Loskiel*, P. 1., p. 159.

flows, and the faith endured unbroken to the end, who have questioned the precious story. They have said as was said before, even of the Divine Master, that humanity in its credulity and dependence upon such noble examples, had created out of its own imagination this story of "The Man and the Sorrowless Tree"—the salvation of our Commonwealth from the universal wrong to that unfortunate race; more incredulous than the unbelievers themselves, they have sought to set aside the simple truth of the tradition, and its lesson most valuable for our example and instruction, was lost to their narrower scrutinies; but none the less therefore, has the story been repeated from generation to generation and preserved in that secure treasure-house of Earth's most valuable possession —"the credence of our common Humanity."

THE LINKS IN THE CHAIN OF THE TESTIMONY.

The treaty at Shackamaxon, the beacon spot in the History of Pennsylvania, still rests after more than one hundred and seventy years, on an unbroken and unvarying tradition; the incidents in relation to it from time to time, successively developed, verify and never contradict it.—*Memoirs Hist. Soc. of Pa.*

WHEN WILLIAM PENN came here, he had six objects principally in view, and to which his first attention was to be directed.

They were: To organize his government. To visit his co-religionists on the shores of the Delaware in Pennsylvania and New Jersey. *To conciliate the Indians.* To pay his respects to the Governors of New York, who had had the command over Pennsylvania. To fix upon a proper spot to build his capital city. To visit Lord Baltimore, with whom he had differences respecting the limits of his province.[1]

The conciliation of the Indians was a leading object. The evidence of this is found first in THE CONDITIONS or concessions, as they were called, to the purchasers and settlers of his lands in Pennsylvania; they bear date the 11th of July, 1681. To these he not only bound himself,

[1] *H. S. of Pa.*, Vol. III., pp. 193-4.

"This he put aside for the Armor of Righteousness."

but all who chose to follow him, who were not permitted to come as settlers to Pennsylvania, unless they subscribed to those conditions. The Sections relating to the Indians are:

XI. There shall be no buying and selling, be it with Indian, or one among another, of any goods to be exported, but what shall be performed in public market, when such places shall be set apart, or erected, where they shall pass the public stamp or mark; if bad ware, and prized as good, or deceitful in proportion or weight, to forfeit the value, as if good and full weight and proportion, to the Public Treasury of this Province, whether it be the merchandise of the Indian, or that of the Planters.

XII. And forasmuch, as it is usual with the planters to overreach the poor natives of the country, in trade, by goods not being good of the kind, or debased with mixtures, with which they are sensibly aggrieved, it is agreed whatever is sold to the Indians, in consideration of their furs, shall be sold in the market place, and there suffer the test, whether good or bad; if good, to pass; if not good, not to be sold for good, that the natives may not be abused nor provoked.

XIII. That no man shall by any ways or means, in word or deed, affront or wrong any Indian, but shall incur the same penalty of the law as if he had committed it against his fellow planter; and if any Indian shall abuse, in word or deed, any planter of his province, that he shall not be his own judge upon the Indians, but he shall make his complaint to the governor of the province, or his lieutenant, or deputy, or some inferior magistrate near him, who shall, at the utmost of his power, take care with the king of the said Indians that all reasonable satisfaction be made to the said injured planter.

XIV. That all differences, between the planter and the natives shall also be ended by twelve men, that is, by six planters and six natives, that so we may live friendly together as much as in us lieth, preventing all occasions of heart-burning and mischief.

XV. That the Indians shall have liberty to do all things relating to improvement of their ground, and providing sustenance for their families, that any of the planters shall enjoy.[1]

Two months after the date of these concessions, he sent three commissioners to manage his affairs in his Colony, namely: William Crispin, John Bezar, and Nathaniel Allen, and requested them to make a league of peace with the Indians in conformity with the concessions.

His INSTRUCTIONS to them were dated 30th of September, 1681, and are in these words: "Be tender of offending the Indians, let them know that you are come to sit down lovingly among them. Let my letter and conditions with my purchasers about just dealing with

[1] *M. H. S. of Pa.*, Vol. III., P. II., p. 153.

them, be read in their tongue, that they may see we have their good in our eye, equal with our interest; and after reading my letter and the said conditions, then present their kings with what I send them, and make a FRIEND-SHIP AND LEAGUE with them according to these conditions, which carefully observe."[1]

Following these instructions he wrote personally to the Indians, informing them of his intentions, and his direction to his commissioners to treat with them about their lands, and the *league of peace.* He wrote first, October 18th, 1681, as follows:

"MY FRIENDS: There is one great God and power that hath made the world and all things therein, to whom you and I, and all people owe their being, and well-being, and to whom you and I must one day give an account for all that we do in the world. Now this great God hath been pleased to make me concerned in your parts of the world, and the king of the country where I live hath given unto me a great province; but I desire to enjoy it with your love and consent, that we may always live together as neighbors and friends: else what would the great God say to us, who hath made us not to devour and destroy one another, but to live soberly and kindly together in the world. Now I would have you well observe that I am very sensible of the unkindness and unjustice that hath been too much exercised to-

[1] *M. H. S. of Pa.*, Vol. III., P. ii., p. 155.

wards you, by the people of these parts of the world, who sought themselves and to make great advantages by you, rather than be examples of justice and goodness unto you, which I hear hath been matter of trouble to you, and caused great grudgings and animosities, sometimes to the shedding of blood, which hath made the great God angry. But I am not such a man, as is well known in my own country. I shall shortly come to see you myself, at which time we may more largely and freely confer and discourse of these matters. In the meantime I have sent my commissioners to treat with you about land and a firm league of peace."

He wrote to them again, 21st April, 1682, to assure them of his love toward them :

"The great God who is the power and wisdom that made you and me, incline your hearts to righteousness, love and peace. This I send to assure you of my love, and to desire your love of my friends, and when the great God brings me among you, I intend to order all things in such manner that we may all live in love and peace with one another, which I hope the great God will incline both me and you to do. I seek nothing but the honors of his name, and that we who are his workmanship may do that which is well pleasing to him."

He wrote again, 21st June, 1682, that he would only enjoy his land upon friendly terms with them, notwithstanding his grant of their country:

"The great God that made thee and me, and all the

world, incline our hearts to love peace and justice, that we may live friendly together, as becomes the workmanship of the great God. The King of England, who is a great prince, hath, for divers reasons, granted to me a large country in America, which, however, I am willing to enjoy upon friendly terms with thee; and this I will say, that the people who come with me are a just, plain, and honest people, that neither make war upon others, nor fear war from others, because they will be just."

His object, therefore, was to purchase their lands, and make with them a firm league of peace; that he fulfilled both of these intentions the evidence remains.

Tamanen, June 23. 1783.

THE LAND TITLES.

THE land titles which were found recorded and unrecorded in the State Archives some years ago and collated are as follows:

Idquahon, Merkekowon and others, Indyan Sachamakers, 15th July, 1682, to William Penn, Esq., Chief Proprietor of the Province of Pennsylvania for lands at the Falls of the Delaware along the Neshammony, and the Islands in the River Delaware.—*Pa. Arch.*, Vol. I., p. 47.

Tamanen, 23d 4th month, 1683, all his Lands Lying betwixt Pemmapecka and Nessaminehs Creeks, to William Penn Proprietʳ and Governʳ of Pennsylvania.—*Pa. Arch.*, Vol. I., p. 62.

Essepenaike, Swanpees, Okettarickon and Wessapoat, 23d 4th month, 1683, their Lands "lying betwixt Pemmapecka and Nesheminck Creeks, all along upon Nesheminck Creek and backward of same, and to Run Two days Journey with an Horse up into ye Country as ye sᵈ River doeth goe," To William Penn, Proprietʳ and

Govern' of ye Province of Pensilvania.—*Pa. Arch.*, Vol. I., p. 63.

Wingebone, 25th 4th month, 1683, all his Lands Lying on ye west side of ye Skolkill River begining from ye Falls of ye same all along upon ye s^d River and Backward of ye same, so farr as my right goeth, to William Penn, Propriet' and Govern' of Pennsilvania.—*Pa. Arch.*,Vol. I., p. 65.

Secane & Icquoquehan, 14th 5th mo., 1683, Lands Lying between Manaiunk als Schulkill and Macopanackhan, als Chester Rivers, begining on ye West side of Manaiunk, thence to ye s^d River Macopanackhan, unto William Penn, Propriet' & Govern' of ye Province of Pennsilvania.—*Pa. Arch.*, Vol. I., p. 65.

Neneshickan, Malebore, 14th 5th mo., 1683, Lands betwixt Manaiunk and Pemmapecka, So farr as ye hill called Consohockin, on ye sayd River Manaiunk, from thence by a Northwest Line to ye River of Pemmapecka unto William Penn, Propriet' and Govern' of ye Province of Pennsilvania.—*Pa. Arch.*, Vol. I., p. 66.

Kekelappan, of Opasiskunk, 10th 7th mo., 1683, unto William Penn, Proprietary & Govern' of ye Province of Pennsilvania, &c., that half of all my Lands betwixt Susquahanna & Delaware, which lyeth on ye Susquehanna side.—*Pa. Arch.*, Vol. I., p. 67.

Machaloha, 18th Oct., 1683, Lands on Delaware River, Chesapeek Bay, and up to ye Falls of Sussquahana River unto William Penn Proprietary & Govern' of ye [Province] of Pennsilvania.—*Pa. Arch.*, Vol. I., p. 67.

Deed from Manghongsin, June 3d, 1684, for all his land upon Pahkehoma, (Perkeomink, now Perkioming. This deed is not recorded.)—*Laws of Pa.*, Vol. II., p. 111.

June 7th, 1684. Richard Mettamicont, calling himself owner of the land on both sides of Pemmapecka creek, on the river Delaware, releases to William Penn. Not recorded.—*Laws of Pa.*, Vol. II., p. 111.

Shakhoppoh, Secane, Malibor, Tangoras, 30th 5th mo., 1685, Lands lying between Macopanackan, als Upland, now called Chester River or Creek, and the River or Creek of Pemapecka, North-Westerly back into ye Woods, to make up Two full Daies Journey, as far as a man can go in Two Dayes, from the said Station.—*Pa. Arch.*, Vol. I., p. 92–3.

Lare, Packenah, Tareekham, 2nd 8th mo., 1685, Lands from Quing Quingus Called Duck Creek unto Upland Called Chester Creek all along by the West Side of Delaware River and So betweene the Said Creeks Backwards as far as a man can Ride in two days with a horse, unto Cap[t] Thomas Holme ye use of William Penn Esq[r] Proprietary & Govern[r] of ye afores[d] Province & Territories.—*Pa. Arch.*, Vol. I., p. 95.

In this place should follow a deed alleged to have existed, dated August 20th, 1686, for the walking purchase, and which occasioned much controversy, and dissatisfaction among the Indians; it is, however, referred to, included in, and confirmed by the deed of August, 1737. It is certain no such original deed was in existence at the treaty of Easton, in 1757.—*Laws of Pa.*, Vol. II., p. 111.

The 15th day of June 1692. King Taminent, Tangorus, Swampes, Hickoqueon. Tract lying between Neshaminah & Poquessing upon the River Delaware, backwards to the utmost bounds of the said province.—*Pa. Arch.*, Vol. I., p. 116–17.

Thos. Dongan to William Penn, 12th January, 1696, consideration, of one hundred Pounds. Tract Lyeing, on both sides the Susquehanah River and the Lakes adjacent, which the said Thomas Dongan, purchased of or had given by the Sinneca Susquehanah Indians, for the end and term of One Thousand years, paying unto the said Thomas Dongan, every year on the Feast day of St. Michaell, the Arch Angell, the rent of a pepper Corn.—*Pa. Arch.*, Vol. I., p. 121–2.

Thos. Dongan to Wm. Penn, 13th January, 1696, for One Hundred Pounds, tract on both sides of the Susquehanah river, beginning at the head of the said River, and running as farr, into the Bay of Chesapeake, purchased of, or had given him by the Sinnica Susquehanah Indians.—*Pa. Arch.*, Vol. I., p. 122–3.

Taminy, Sachimack, Weheeland, and Weheequeckhon, who is to be king after my death, Yaqueekhon, and Quenameckquid, my Sonns, 5th July, 1697, unto William Penn, Lands, Between the Creek called Pemopeck, and the Creek called Neshaminy, in the said Province from the River Delaware, so farr as a horse can Travel in Two Summer dayes.—*Pa. Arch.*, Vol. I., p. 124–5.

Widaagh, Andaggy-junkquagh, Kings, of the Susquehannagh Indians, 13th Sep., 1700, unto William Penn, the River Susquehannagh, and all the Islands therein, and all the Lands lying upon both sides of the River, next adjoyning to ye same, extending t< the utmost confines of the Lands.—*Pa. Arch.*, Vol. I., p. 133.

Articles of agreement between William Penn, and the Susquehanna, Shawona, Potowmack, and Conestogoe Indians, dated April 23d, 1701. (Recorded in Book F, Vol. III., page 43.) Among other things they ratify and confirm Governor Dongan's deed of January, 1696, and the above deed of the Susquehanna Indians, of September, 1700.

A deed of release, 17th of September, 1718, from sundry Delaware Indian Chiefs, viz.: Sassoonah, Meetashechay, Ghettypeneeman, Pokehais, Ayamackan, Opekasset, and Pepawmamam, for all the lands situate between the two rivers, Delaware and Susquehanna, from Duck creek to the mountains on this side Lechay. This deed is recorded, May 13th, 1728, in Book A, Vol. VI., page 59.

Sasooaam, Sachem of the Schuylkill Indians, in Pensilvania; Elalapis, Ohopamen, Pesqueetomen, Mayeenrol, Partridge, Tepakoaset alias Joe, on behalf of our Selves and all the other Indians of the said Nation, 7th Sep., 1732, unto John Penn, Thomas Penn & Richard Penn, land lying on the River Schuylkill, between the Lechaig Hills and Keekachtanemin Hills, which cross the River Thirty

Miles above the Lechaig Hills, all Land whatsoever lying within the said bounds and between the bran hes of Delaware River on the Eastern side of said Land, and the streams running into the Susquehannah on the Western side of the said Land.—*Pa. Arch.*, Vol. I., p. 347.

Previous, however, to this treaty, there appears to have been a release, but not recorded, from sundry Indians, for all the land on both sides of the Brandywine creek. This release is dated May 31st, 1726. Ratified by Lingahonoa, a Schuylkill Indian, who was not present at signing the foregoing deed, 12th July, 1742. Confirmed by deed of release, 20th of August, 1733, for the consideration of said lands received by them. This release is also confirmed by Lingahonoa, 12th July, 1742, acknowledging that he had received his portion of the consideration. These deeds and releases have never been recorded.—*Laws of Pa.*, Vol. II., p. 114.

Chiefs of the Nations of ye Onondagoes; Senekaes; Cayoogoes; and Tuskaroras; 11th Oct., 1736, release to John Penn, Thomas Penn and Richard Penn, all the River Susquehannah, with the Lands lying on both sides thereof, to Extend Eastward as far as the heads of the Branches or Springs, which run into the said Susquehannah, And on the west side of the River, to the setting of the Sun, to extend from the mouth of the said River Northward, the same to the hills or mountains called the Tyanuntasacta, or Endless hills.—*Pa. Arch.*, Vol. I., p. 494-5.

The Indian chiefs on their return, staid several days with Conrad Weiser, at Tulpehocken, and there executed the following deed, dated October 25th, 1736, which is proved and recorded in Book C., Vol. II., p. 350, May 22d, 1741.—*Laws of Pa.*, Vol. II., p. 115.

The Chiefs of the Six Nations, the Onandagoes, Isanundowans or Sinnekas, Cayoogoes, Oneydas, Tuscaroras, (in behalf also of ye Canyingoes or Mohacks,) 11th Oct., 1736, release to John Penn, Thomas Penn, and Richard Penn, Propriettors of Pennsylvania, and to their Heirs and successors, All their Right, to the Lands on both sides of the River Sasquehannah.—*Pa. Arch.*, Vol. I., p. 498.

There is an indorsement of ratification on this deed, dated 9th of July, 1754, signed by nine Indians.

August 25th, 1737. Teshakomen, *alias* Tishekunk, and Nootamis *alias* Nutimus, two of the sachemas, or chiefs of the Delaware Indians, several tracts of land, which their forefathers had more than fifty years ago, bargained and sold unto their good friend and brother William Penn, the father of the said John and Thomas Penn, and in particular one deed from the chiefs or kings of the northern Indians on Delaware, release to the proprietors and desire it may be walked, travelled, or gone over by persons appointed for that purpose. Recorded May 8th, 1741, in book G., Vol. I., p. 282.

The sachems of the Indian nation called Onontagers, Sinickers, Mohocks; or Oneyders, Cayiukers, Tuscor-

rorow, Shomoken, the Delawares, Shawanes; the 22d
day of August, 1749, consideration of £500, that tract
or parcel of land, called in the language of the Five
Nation Indians Tyanuntasachta, or endless hills, and by
the Delaware Indians Kekactany hills, east side of the
river Susquenna, and from thence running up the said
river to the nearest mountain, to the north side of the
creek called Cantaguy, and from thence to the main
branch of Delaware river, at the creek Lechawachsein,
and from thence down the river Delaware to the Kekachtany hills aforesaid, and from thence to the place
of beginning. Recorded May 6th, 1752, in book H,
Vol. II., p. 204.—*Laws of Pa.*, Vol. II., p. 119.

Deed dated July 6th, 1754, from the sachems, of the
Mohock nation, the Oneydo, Onondago, Cayuga, Seneca
and Tuscarora Indians, in consideration of £400 to
Thomas and Richard Penn, the lands beginning at the
Kittochtinny or Blue hills, on the west branch of Susquehanna river, and thence by the said, a mile above the
mouth of a certain creek, called Kayarondinhagh; thence
far as the province of Pennsylvania extends its western
lines or boundaries; thence along said western line to
the south line of said province; thence to the south side
of the said Kittochtinny hills; thence to the place of
beginning.—*Laws of Pa.*, Vol. II., p. 120.

Deed of October 23d, 1758, from the chiefs of the
Mohock nation, Onondago nation, Seneca nation, the
Oneyda nation, Cayuga nation, & Tuscarora nation, re-

citing a deed poll, bearing date, the 6th day of July, 1754; a treaty held at Easton, on the 23d October, & the amicable settlement of boundaries between the aforesaid sachems and chiefs and Richard Peters and Conrad Weiser, esqs., &c., for the Proprietors. Recorded in book I, Vol. IV., p. 488, September 5th, 1768.—*Laws of Pa.*, Vol. II., p. 121.

The last purchase of the proprietaries from the Indians, was made at Fort Stanwix, November 5th, 1768, Recorded at Philadelphia, in the Roll's Office in book of deeds, No. 3, p. 23, July 12th, 1781.—*Laws of Pa.*, Vol. II., p. 122.

At the treaty at Fort Stanwix on October 23, 1784, a purchase was made of the residue of the Indian land within the limits of Pennsylvania, and the deed signed by the chiefs of the Six Nations.

At a treaty held at Fort M'Intosh, with the Wyandott and Delaware Indians, by the same commissioners, January, 1785, a deed was executed by those nations, for the same lands, in the same words, with the same boundaries, which deed is dated January 21st, 1785. Both these deeds, with the treaties, or conferences, are printed at large, in the journals of the assembly, in the appendix to the journal of the session of February—April, 1785.

Thus, in a period of about one hundred and two years the whole right of soil of the Indians, within the charter bounds of Pennsylvania, was extinguished, by purchase from them.—*Laws of Pa.*, Vol. II., p. 123.

The founder's intention was therefore carried out as far as the purchase of the Ind'an titles; and it must be remembered in this connection that he alone with but rare exceptions, among all, whether Governments, nations or individuals who took possession of the Continent recognized the Indian Title. It must be further remem— bered that he made not one purchase, nor from one tribe, nor for the whole State at any one time, but from every tribe which claimed possession, and that the con-

On the 3d of October, 1788, an act was passed entitled, an act to authorize the supreme executive council to draw on the state treasurer for a sum of money, for defraying the expense of purchasing of the Indians, lands on lake Erie (chap. 1355.) By which act a sum of £1200 was granted to purchase the Indian rights, in the lake Erie tract, bargained to be sold by the United States of Pennsylvania, and a further grant was added for the same purpose, by an act of the 28th of September, 1789, (chap. 1439.)

The Indian cession of the Presque Isle lands, is dated January 9th, 1789, and is in these words.—The signing chiefs do acknowledge the right of soil, and jurisdiction to, and over that tract of country bounded on the south by the north line of the State of Pennsylvania, on the east by the west boundary of the State of New York, agreeable to the cession of that State and Massachusetts to the United States, and on the north by the margin of lake Erie, including Presque Isle; and all the bays and harbours along the margin of lake Erie, from the west boundary of Pennsylvania, to where the west boundary of the State of New York may cross or intersect the south margin of the said lake Erie, to be vested in the said State of Pennsylvania, agreeable to an act of Congress dated the 6th of June last, (1788.)

By an act of the 13th of April, 1791, (chap. 1556) the governor was authorized to complete the purchase from the United States, which, according to a communication from him to the legislature, was done in March, 1792; and the consideration money, amounting to 151,640 dollars and twenty-five cents, paid in continental certificates, of various descriptions. The deed of confirmation from the United States is dated March 3d, 1792, which is recorded in the Roll's Office in deed book No. 31, p. 107, April 25, 1792.—*Laws of Pa.*, Vol. II., p. 123-4.

sideration aggregated a large amount altogether[1]—with what he paid in every way from first to last exhausting his inheritance from his father and his whole available possessions; and that he continued his policy in his successors. Many strings of beads which was their only money, many fathoms of Stroud waters which was their better clothing, many hoes and axes which were their first implements for less toilsome labor for their women; in a word, whatever had value for their purposes in very adequate quantities. The deeds from the Indian Aborigines cited above and which were rescued from the unrecorded waste in our State Archives years afterwards were by no means the whole number;[2] the

[1] "My profit by the Indians was never sixpence, but my known perpetual bounties to them have cost me many hundreds of pounds, if not some thousands first and last."—*Penn's Answer P. & L. Corr.*, Vol. I., p. 27.

He sometimes repurchased the same property from another tribe—of which the following was a notable instance:

At his first coming over late in November, 1682 (40 years prior to 1722), he went to New York and got some persons to purchase the lands on the Susquehanna from the five nations who claimed them by right of conquest—for which he sent a great many goods in a vessel to New York, yet such was his sense of equity that when he found those living on the lands "were sorry," he lay the parchments on the ground before them to signify that the ground was again free to all once more as before, and then entered into a new agreement and repurchased from them the same land.—*An Enquiry*, London, 1759.

The Indian deed to Colonel Dongan is not known to exist, nor is there any trace of it in the public offices. It is known, however, that he was the agent of William Penn to make the purchase.—*Laws of Pa.*, Vol. II., p. 111.

[2] A list of Indian purchases, in which these deeds appear, was made out before 1759 by Charles Thomson as follows:

Second October, 1683, lands on Duck Creek; 12th January, 1696, on the Susquehanna; 13th September, 1700, on the Susquehanna; 5th July, 1697, on the Pennepack; 23rd April, 1701, which were Articles of Friendship and agreement with

most important paper described in this volume among very many others and having no representation but the envelope in which it was enclosed. It must also be considered that the Founder was obliged to release his father's large claim on the British Government, for the British title which was more valueless than that of the Aborigines; a title neither based on conquest, nor occupancy, nor discovery, and which was made wholly worthless within a Century by the Settlers themselves; that the title of the Indians was neither initiated by the exclusive occupancy of one tribe, nor completed by the expenditure of labor upon the ground, but existed only in the vagrant holding of whatever tribe held temporary advantage over another. That the land itself was without value until made valuable by the labor of his followers, to which heart, spirit and purpose was given by the wise and humane direction of the Founder. From which facts result, as it does always in the most valuable work for humanity, that every one received compensatory advantages, except the Founder, who was himself

William Penn; 17th September, 1718, Duck Creek to Lechay; 11th October, 1736, Release of Susquehanna lands; 25th October, 1736, Lands South of Kittocktanny Hills; 25th Aug., 1737, Deed from Pitcocks falls west; 23rd July, 1748, Articles of Friendship between the chiefs of the Tweghtwees and the government of Pennsylvania; 22nd Aug., 1749, Release of land between Kictocktinny and Maghuinoy; 6th July, 1754, Release of lands west side of the Susquehanna; 9th July, 1754, Indorsement on Deed.

At the time this list was made, "there was a considerable number of other Indian deeds in the hands of the Secretary for lands purchased at several times particularly in 1732-3, but which they would never record nor would they produce."—*An Enquiry*, London, 1759. H. S. Lib.

brought to ruin by his wise and honest endeavor, and his whole establishment finally lost to his family.[1]

[1] In a letter in 1684 he says: And thou Philadelphia, the Virgin settlement named before thou wert born, what love, what care, what service, and what travail, has there been to bring thee forth, and preserve thee, from such as would defile thee.

In a letter to James Logan, 8th 6th mo., 1704, he says: O Pennsylvania what hast thou cost me? Above £30,000 more than I ever got by it; two hazardous and most fatiguing voyages; my straights and slavery here.

Another letter, 14th 7th mo., 1705, on the account of settling and maintaining the colony I spent £10,000 the first two years as appears by my accounts here, £3,000 overspent in King James' time and no supply coming from Pennsylvania. The vast sum of money also I have melted away here in London.—*Gordon's History*, 607–8.

The survey of Mason and Dixon in 1762 cost the Penn Family $100,000.—*Hist of Erie Co.*, p. 58.

The Wampum Belt.

THE GREAT TREATY.

SUCH was the execution of his first object in coming to the province—to treat with them about land.

The evidence that he executed his second purpose —"to live on friendly terms with thee"—to make "the firm league of peace"—is no less conclusive. We might reason *a priori*, that he would the more certainly have executed this latter purpose.

He who placed the true and loving lives of all humanity above money considerations, would not have been satisfied with the simple barter of beads, few or many, of little value to him, for ground, whether measured by inches or strode over by day's journeys, for men or horses, of as little value to them, but would have sought these Aboriginese as he did the poor and humble everywhere, and made peace between God and him and them in this only way—the pledge of, and the living of, true lives to each other.

What was of the most real importance to him was that brotherly love should continue between them and him, and every one. Lands and money and titles were his by his inheritance, but he preferred to walk the Lon-

(36)

don streets breadless, to go to the tower and to death, if thereby he might keep his protest on his head, against cant, and war, and the inhumanity of men to each other.

But the assurance that he carried out the second purpose rests neither on its probabilities, nor tradition only —but the records of the history of his work, which we now cite here.

COUNCIL AT PHILADELPHIA, 16th June, 1718.

The old League of friendship renewed. The Chief of the Conestogoa Indians, the Shawnois above Conestogoe, Ganawais & Delawares, waited on the Governr. & Council; the Captain of the Conestogoes, said they were on a ffriendly visit to Renew the old League of ffriendship that had hitherto been between us and them,

Post Meridiem,

The Governr. Ordered the Interpreters to Deliver them what follows in writing,

That their ffriendly visit on a Design to Brighten & Strengthen the Chain which had for so many years bound & united them & this Governmt. together as one People, was very acceptable. They were sensible that William Penn, Lord of this Country, had been as a Common ffather to them; he had Given it in Charge to all those who Governed in his stead, to treat them in the same ffriendly manner he had Done himself.—*Col. Rec.*, Vol. III., page 38.

COUNCIL AT PHILADELPHIA, July the 12th, 1720.

James Logan, Secretary, reported to the Board, That

the Governour had desired him to proceed to Sasquehannah, and their discourse the Indians. That he went; That the Chiefs of the Mingoes, the Shawanese, the Ganawese, and some of the Delawares, met him; the Mingoes spoke as follows,

That when Governour Penn first held Councils with them, he promised them so much Love and Friendship that he would not call them Brothers, because Brothers might differ, nor Children because these might offend and require Correction, but he would reckon them as one Body, and Blood, one Heart and one Head; But few of the old men who were at those Councils were living; These were removed, and those who were then very young are now grown up to succeed, but they transmitted it to their Children, and they and all theirs should remember it forever;

<small>William Penn's promises at the first Treaty.</small>

The Ganawese say, That their present Chief was once at Council with William Penn before they removed into this province, and that since they came into it, they have always lived quiet and in Peace, When the Sun sets they sleep in Peace and in Peace they rise with him, and so continue while he continues his course, and think themselves happy in their Friendship, which they shall take Care to have continued from Generation to Generation.

The Conestogoes say, That William Penn made a League with them to last for three or four Generations; That he is now dead, and most of their ancients are also dead, but the League

<small>William Penn made a league with them to last for three or four generations.</small>

still remains, and they take this Opportunity to renew and strengthen it with their ffriend. One Generation may die, and another may die, but the League of Friendship continues strong and shall forever continue.

The Indians being met again the Secretary spoke to them as follows: It must be a great Satisfaction to all honest and good men, to find that the measures that great man Wm. Penn, took to establish a firm Friendship with you has had such excellent Success. You on your parts have been faithful and true unto us, the Chain was still preserved strong and bright. You never violated it.

We have lived in perfect Peace and Unity above any other Government in America; you renewing the Chain at this time upon the Decease of your great Friend, with us who remain alive, is so affectionate and kind that I shall not fail to represent it duly to the Governour and your good Friends in Philadelphia. This Chain has been made near forty years agoe; It is at this time strong and bright as ever, and I hope will continue so between our Children and your Children, and their Children's Children to all Generations, while the water flows or the sun shines in the Heavens.—*Col. Rec.*, Vol. III., page 88.

<small>The Treaty was made near 40 years before 1720 (1682).</small>

A COUNCIL AT PHILADELPHIA, July the 19th, 1720.

William Keith Esqr., The Governour presented the Draught of a Letter to the President of New York, as follows:

Philadelphia, July 19th, 1720. When Governour Penn first settled this Country, he made it his Chief Care to cultivate a strict Alliance and Friendship with all the Indians; when he came to treat with the Indians settled upon the River Sasquehannah, finding that they accounted themselves a Branch of the Mingoes or ffive Nations, he prevailed with Colonel Dongan, the Governour of New York, to treat with those Nations in his behalf, and to purchase from them all their claim of Right to the Lands on both sides of Sasquehannah, which Colonel Dongan did accordingly; and for a valuable consideration paid in Sterling money, Colonel Dongan, by good Deeds transferr'd or convey'd his said Right purchased from the Five Nations to Governour Penn & his Heirs, in due Form of Law.

Upon Governour Penn's last arrival here, about twenty years agoe, he held a Treaty with the Mingoes or Conestogoe Indians settled on Sasquehannah; their Chiefs, did then not only acknowledge the Sale of those Lands made to Colonel Dongan as above, but as much as in them lay did also renew and confirm the same to Governour Penn.—*Col. Rec.*, Vol. III., page 95.

[sidenote: Another Treaty made 20 years prior to 1720.]

COUNCIL AT PHILADELPHIA, March the 21st, 1721. Sir William Keith, Bart., Governour. James Logan & Colonel John French report they met with the Chiefs of the Mingoe or Conestogoe Indians, of the Shawanese & Ganawese, and some of the Dela-

[sidenote: A reference to the First Treaty.]

wares in Council, and spoke to them in the following Words; William Penn our and your Father, when he first settled this Country with English Subjects, made a firm League of Friendship and Brotherhood with all the Indians then in these parts, and agreed that both you and his People should be all as one Flesh and Blood. The same League has often been renewed by himself and other Governours under him, with their Councils, held as well in this place where we now are as at Philadia. and other places. His People and yours have hitherto inviolably observed these Leagues.

And to the Messenger we delivered the following Words as the signification of the Belt we sent with him, viz: Deliver this Belt from the Governour and Government of Pennsilvania to the King or Chief of the Sinnekaes, and say that the words it brings are these. William Penn made a firm Peace and League with the Indians in these parts near forty years agoe, which League has often been renewed and never broken.—*Col. Rec.*, Vol. III., page 152.

<small>William Penn made a Treaty near 40 years prior to 1721 (1682).</small>

COUNCIL AT CONESTOGOE, July the 7th, 1721. Sir William Keith, Bart., Governour. Ghesaont, on the behalf of all the ffive Nations delivered himself as follows: They were glad to see the Governour and his Council at this place, they find him to be their Friend and Brother, and the same as if William Penn was still amongst them. They assure the Governour and Council that they had not forgot William Penn's Treaties with them, and that his advice to them was still fresh in their memories. Though they cannot write, yet they retain every thing said in their Councils with all the Nations they treat with, and preserve it as carefully in their memories as if it was committed in our method to Writing.—*Col. Rec.*, Vol. III., page 119.

COUNCIL AT CONESTOGOE, July the 8th, 1721.

Sir William Keith Bart., Governour spoke to them in these Words.

I am glad to find that you remember what William Penn formerly said to you; He was a great and a good man, his own People loved him; He loved the Indians, and they also loved him, Though he is now removed from us, yet his children and people following his Example will always take the same measures, So that his and our posterity will be as a long chain of which He was the first Link, and when one link ends another succeeds, and then another, being all firmly bound together in one strong chain to endure for ever.—*Col. Rec.*, Vol. III., page 122.

COUNCIL AT THE INDIAN TOWN OF CONESTOGOE, May 26th, 1728.

Chiefs of the Conestogoe Indians, some of the Delawares on Brandywine, Ganawese Indians & Shawanese. Patrick Gordon, The Govr. Spoke as follows: My Friends and Brethren: You are sensible that the Great William Penn, the Father of this Country, when he first brought his People with him over the broad Sea, took all the Indians the old Inhabitants by the hand, & because he found them to be a sincere honest People he took them to his heart & loved them as his own. He then made a strong League & Chain of Friendship with them, by which it was agreed that the Indians & the English, with all the Christians, should be as one People. Your Friend & Father William Penn still retained a warm Affection for all the Indians, & strictly commanded those whom he sent to govern this People to treat the Indians as their Children, & continued in this kind love for them until his Death.

<small>He made a league when he first brought his people over.</small>

His Sons have now sent me over in their Stead, & they gave me strict Charge to love all the Indians as their Brethren, & as their Father William Penn loved you.

I am now come to see you, and to renew the ancient Friendship which has been between William Penn's People and you, the Conestogoes, Delawares, Ganawese and Shawanese Indians upon Sasquehannah.

My Brethren:

You have been faithful to your Leagues with us, your Hearts have been clean, & you have preserved the Chain from Spotts or Rust, or if there are any you have been carefull to wipe them away; your Leagues with you Father William Penn, & with his Governours are in Writing on Record, that our Children & our Childrens Children may have them in everlasting Remembrance. And we know that you preserve the memory of those things amongst you by telling them to your Children, & they again to the next Generation, so that they remain stamp'd on your Minds never to be forgott.

The Chief Heads or strongest Links of this Chain I find are these Nine, vizt.:

<small>The Chief heads of the Treaty he then made were</small>

1st. "That all William Penns People or Christians, and all the Indians should be brethren, as the Children of one Father, joyned together as with one Heart, one Head & one Body.

2nd. "That all Paths should be open and free to both Christians and Indians.

3rd. "That the Doors of the Christians Houses should be open to the Indians & the Houses of the Indians open to the Christians, & that they should make each other welcome as their Friends.

4th. "That the Christians should not believe any false Rumours or Reports of the Indians, nor the Indians believe any such Rumors or Reports of the Christians, but should first come as Brethren to enquire of each other; And that both Christians & Indians, when they hear any such false Reports of their Brethren, they should bury them as in a bottomless Pitt.

5th. "That if the Christians heard any ill news that may be to the Hurt of the Indians, or the Indians hear any such ill news that may be to the Injury of the Christians, they should acquaint each other with it speedily as true Friends & Brethren.

6th. "That the Indians should do no manner of Harm

to the Christians nor their Creatures, nor the Christians do any Hurt to any Indians, but each treat the other as their Brethren.

7th. "But as there are wicked People in all Nations, if either Indians or Christians should do any harm to each other, Complaint should be made of it by the Persons Suffering that Right may be done, & when Satisfaction is made, the Injury or Wrong should be forgott & be buried as in a bottomless Pitt.

8th. "That the Indians should in all things assist the Christians, & the Christians assist the Indians against all wicked People that would disturb them.

9th. "And lastly, that both Christians & Indians should acquaint their Children with this League & firm Chain of Friendship made between them, & that it should always be made stronger & stronger & be kept bright & clean, without Rust or Spott between our Children and Childrens Children, while the Creeks and Rivers run, and while the Sun, Moon & Stars endure.

"My Brethren:

"I have now spoke to the League and Chain of Friendship, first made by your Father William Penn with your Fathers, which is confirmed."—*Col. Rec.*, Vol. III., pages 329–30.

COUNCIL AT PHILADELPHIA, June 4th, 1728.

Patrick Gordon, Esqr., Lieut. Governr. and the King of the Delawares, five Nations & a Shawanese. The Governour spoke as follows:

When your Great Father William Penn's Children sent me hither, they commanded me to love & be kind to the Indians as their Brethren, I appointed a Meeting, at which I desired the other Chiefs might be present, that we might all together, as Friends and Brethren, renew and strengthen the Chain of Friendship which your Father William Penn made with all the Indians of this Province, that it may be kept bright forever.

<small>All the Indians of the province were r presented at the Treaty.</small>

About ten days since I mett the Indians of Conestogoe, the Shawanese, Ganawese, & divers of the Delawares at Conestogoe town, we then opened our Hearts, we spoke as Brethren & Friends, we brightened the Chain & made it strong, that it might last & continue firm, while the Sun & Moon endure.

We then went over all the Heads, the strong Links of the Chain made between your Father William Penn & the Indians, we keep them in writing, that they may be had in everlasting Remembrance, the Indians also keep them in their Memory & in their Hearts, they tell them to their Children, & these tell them again to their Children, that from Generation to Generation they may be remembered forever. These are the Chief Points of those Treaties that were first made by William Penn with your Fathers, & have since from time to time been confirmed.

(The nine Heads or Links mentioned in the Treaty of Conestogoe were repeated.)—*Col Rec.*, Vol. III., page 334-5.

AT THE COURTHO. OF PHILADIA., October 10th, 1728.

Patrick Gordon, Esqr., Lieut. Governr. present, also Sassoonan & Chiefs of the Delawares, five Nations, Brandywine Indians, with several others.

Sassoonan, spoke as follows: That when their Father, William Penn, was in this country, it was agreed that both Christians and Indians should joyn in removing all Difficulties, & if any Stone or Stump should ly in the Way, that both should joyn their Hands together & help to remove it, that old men & Children might walk safely.—*Col. Rec.*, Vol. III., page 353.

October 11th.

The Governour spoke to them in these Words: As you are now come, tho' few in Number Yet in the Name of all the Delawares, Shawanese, & Mingoes, amongst us, to declare your Friendship, & their resolution to live in Peace unto the Christians forever, I will again goe over the Links of the Chain made between William Penn and you, which I repeated to my Brethren at Conestogoe in the Summer, that they may be the more fresh in your Minds, because you have no Writing amongst you, & I desire that you may repeat them over and over again to your Children, & to all your People, & to all the Indians that live amongst you, that you may have them at all times stamp'd on your Hearts and fixed in your View."

The links of the chain taken up and gone over again by Governor Gordon.

(Here the nine Articles or Links of the Chain, as in the Treaty held at Conestogoe, were repeated.)—*Col. Rec.*, Vol. III., pages 255–6.

Council at Philada., May 26th, 1729.

Tawenna stood up & said: He never spoke since William Penn was here till last Spring, & he now speaks the same again to the Governour, That William Penn in his house in this town, told them they must be one Body & he now says the same; they are not to be as People bound together to each other, tho' the Bonds were ever so strong, tho' they were of Iron, for even in that case the one may suffer & the other escape, but they & we, as William Penn said, must be as the same Body, half the one & half the other, that cannot be divided, that each may both have Joy & Pain alike, as the same Body without any Division. William Penn said that as both Nations were to be the same Body, so if by any stroke that Body were to be divided down the middle into two parts so that they fell assunder, This should be looked upon as the act of Providence, which neither could help or be blamed for.

William Penn further said, that if all the People around us should differ one with another, yet we must not differ but continue the same in Love and Peace; that the Indians ought not hastily to goe out to War but rather should study Peace, & that if they were attacked he & his People would be ready to defend them, for that we are all as one People. William Penn told the Indians that he loved them all, their Men, Women & Children, and that he held Councils with them to perpetuate the

<small>Fairman or Lass Cock's house where the writing was signed.</small>

Remembrance of his Affection towards them, that the Friendship he had established with them was to last for many Generations; that their old Men die & others come in their Room, who likewise die, but that the Love & Friendship between the English & Indians ought to remain forever.—*Col. Rec.*, Vol. III., pages 383–85.

That William Penn is dead, but he now repeats all these things to the Governour whom he looks upon as in his stead, & as if William Penn himself were alive; that he remembers all these things which were then said, and He has now spoke in the Name of the Conestogoe, Ganawese, Delaware, & Shawanese Indians.— *Col. Rec.*, Vol. III., page 386.

COUNCIL AT PHILADIA., May 27th, 1729.

Patrick Gordon, Esqr., Lieut. Governr. And the same Indians as before, The Governour spoke in these words: I am glad to find by your Discourse, that you not only remember what I said to you last Spring, but also there are some yet living amongst you who can remember what your Father William Penn said to your People when he was in the Countrey, from thence you see that His Words & mine are the same. He agreed with all the Indians whom he treated with in the several Points that I laid before you at Conestogoe: they were his Words, tho' spoken by me, & as I observe the old Men well remember them; so now I desire you again to repeat them over to your Children & require them to remember them & to repeat

<small>Governor Gordon repeats again the words of the first Treaty which they remember.</small>

them again to their Children, that the same may be continued not only to your Children but through all Generations & to all Ages.

By this means we shall truely continue not only Friends & Brothers, but one People, of one Body, one Mind & one Heart. We shall rejoyce together & be sorrowfull together, & we shall all be the same.—*Col. Rec.*, Vol. III., pages 386–87.

Letter of Gov. Gordon to Delaware Indians, 1731, at Alleghening:

<small>Reference to the first treaty again.</small> I find that when your father William Penn first came into this Country he called all the Indians together and made a strong chain & league of friendship with them, which was that He and his People and they and their People & their Children and Children's Children & their Children and so forward to all ages and generations, should be one people as of the same flesh and blood and the same body as long as the Waters should flow and the Sun, Moon and Stars endure. And William Penn gave it always in Charge to all his Governours whom he sent into this Country in his stead to be kind to all the Indians as his Brethren and Children, and accordingly all the Governours of this place have from time to time renew'd the same Treaty and brightned the Chain with all the Indians and we have lived and doe live as true friends and brethren. If any white man hurt an Indian he is punished for it, and you have heard that some of our people have been hang'd

on a Gallows for being wicked to the Indians. I wrote the Order for it and they were putt to death because they had abused our brethren.—*Pa. Arch.*, Vol. I., p. 303.

COUNCIL HELD AT PHILADELPHIA, August 23d, 1732.

Thomas Penn, Esqr., Proprietary. James Logan, Isaac Norris, Samuel Preston, Samuel Hasell, Thomas Laurence, Esq'rs. Present also: Chiefs of the Tsanandowas: Chiefs of the Cayooges, & Oneidas; The Proprietor, spoke as follows ;

<small>Thomas Penn renews the league first made by his father.</small>

I need not inform you that when my Father, William Penn, was Sent by the Great King of England to bring over large Numbers of his People to settle in this Country, he made it his first and principal Care to convince all the Indians inhabiting it, that he came with a full Design to be their Friend and Benefactor.

And he entered into the Strictest League of Amity with them, not only between himself and his People and the Indians then living, but to continue between his Children and their Children and their Posterity to all Generations, & for this Purpose he made with them a Chain of Friendship, to be kept Strong and bright forever. And when his Affairs in England obliged him to leave this Country, he gave it strictly in Charge to all his Governors and People in Power under him, that they should in the same manner treat all the Indians as he had done; That they should be as Fathers to them, & that all his People should live in perfect Peace and Brotherhood with all the Indians, as if they were of one Blood and one Body, without distinction.

I am but young, and having been bred in England could not see those things with my own Eyes, but I Constantly had Accounts in writing of all that was done here, as if I had been myself in the Place, and by reading these over again I now know them better than if I had been present, and were to be informed by Memory only, so that I can fully speak to them.

And now, since I am here with you my Self, I do assure you that the Friendship & strict Union which my Father began with all our Friends, the Indians, and his Governors after him have cultivated, I shall take Care to improve and strengthen. My Father made a Chain and Covenant for himself and his Children, and I his Son, will to the best of my Power make that Chain yet stronger and brighter on our Parts; that it may continue so to all Generations.—*Col. Rec.*, Vol. III., p. 466.

COUNCIL AT PHILADELPHIA, the Great Meeting house, August 31st, 1732. Thomas Penn, Esqr., Proprietary. A very great Audience, that crowded the House and all its Gallaries. The Chiefs of the Indians all their People who accompanied them in their Journey—The clerk of the Council said, "as we have had several Treaties of Friendship with the Six Nations, & you have always found us steady &

The links of the chain as renewed by Thomas Penn.

constant to you in all we have professed, & we have now upon the Arrival of the Son of their great Friend, William Penn, who first began the Settlement of this Province, a fuller Opportunity than Ever, of freely opening our Hearts to each other. His Son, who has just on his Arrival so happily mett you here, with the Lieutenant Governor and Council, for all the People of this Province, not only renew & confirm all former Treaties, but enter into the most strict & closest League of Friendship, Love & Union with all the Six Nations at first named, desiring that the same Friendship may be extended to all the other Nations," with whom you are or shall be in Alliance, of which these Heads that we are now to mention, are the Chief & ever to be kept in Remembrance:

1st. We shall consider the Six Nations as ourselves, and you shall consider all our inhabitants as your own people.

2d. You shall not believe any false or idle Rumours concerning you, but each shall Enquire of the other into the Truth of what they hear.

3d. If you know or learn any thing that may hurt us, you shall carefully inform us of it, and if we hear any thing that may hurt you, we shall in like manner acquaint you.

4th. If any evil minded Person amongst us should hurt any of your People, they shall be punished as if they had done it to an English Subject, in which you have known some Instances of our Care, and if any of your People hurt any of ours, we shall expect the like justice.

5th. We will constantly keep a Fire for you at Philadelphia, that when any of the Chiefs of your Nations come hither, we may sitt down together round it, and advise and consult of such Affairs as may be for the general interest of both you and us. On this Article was delivered a Belt of Wampum.

6th. And we now desire, there may be an open Road between Philadelphia and the towns of the Six Nations, which we will on our parts, clear from every Grub, Stump & Log, that it may be straight, smooth & free for us and you.

7th. This League and Chain of Friendship & Brotherhood, we now make with all the Six Nations, vizt: the Tsanandowans, Onandagoes, Ganyingoes, Cayoogoes, Oneidas & Tuscarores, for us and our People, and for our Children and Children's Children with you for all your Nations, and for your Children & Children's Children to all Generations, to continue so long as the Heavens, Sun, Moon, Stars, & the Earth shall Endure. And we desire that the same may at your return be ratified & confirmed at your great Fire by all your People, and be kept in perpetual Remembrance, and that all our Indians & all the Nations of Indians in Alliance with you, may be comprehended within the same.

And for the Confirmation hereof, we now make you this Present

Then were delivered the Goods which, by order of the Board were provided by the Treasurer.

The Proprietor was pleased to add to the Present, Six fine jappaned & guilt Guns, which he brought over with him, to be delivered one to the Chief of Each of the Six Nations.

The Indians, on receiving the Belts of Wampum & the Present, expressed their Thankfullness by a harmonious Sound peculiar to them, in which those of each Nation now present joyned alternately, & they repeated the same with great Seeming Satisfaction.—*Col. Rec.*, Vol. III., p. 481.

Directions being given for their Entertainment while they remained in Town, & for providing some necessaries for their Journey, the Indians taking the Proprietor, Governor, & Members of Council by the hand, departed, & thus the Treaty ended.—*Col. Rec.*, Vol. III., pages 482-83.

Council at Philadelphia, Septr. 30th, 1732.

Thomas Penn Esqr., Proprietary. Shawanese Chiefs.

<small>The Treaty of 1701 again referred to.</small> They were then acquainted that a great Treaty had lately been held with the Six Nations, that a considerable Number of their Nation, about thirty-four years since, (as the Govr. told them in his Letter,) coming with their Wives & Families to Settle at Conestogoe, they then entered into a League of Friendship with this Government; first with Coll. Markham, the then Lieutenant Governor, and in about three years after, with

William Penn, himself, who was a Father to all the Indians: that from tl at time the Shawanese became as Brothers to the English, as all our other Indians are.— *Col. Rec.*, Vol. III., pages 491–93.

COUNCIL AT PHILADELPHIA, October 16th, 1734.
Honourable Proprietaries John & Thomas Penn Esqr.
John Penn, Esqr., spoke as follows. I am well pleased Thomas Penn promises to strengthen the league made with his father. with the Opportunity your visit gives me, so soon after my Arrival here, to see my good friends Hetaquantagechty and Shekallamy, of both whom I have received so favourable a Character that you shall always be welcome to me, and I desire you to assure all the Indians, and particularly my good friends of the Six Nations, that it shall be my constant care to strengthen that firm League and Chain of Friendship which my Father first began, and has since been carefully preserved between the Indians and all the People within this Government.—*Col. Rec.*, Vol. III., pages 626–27.

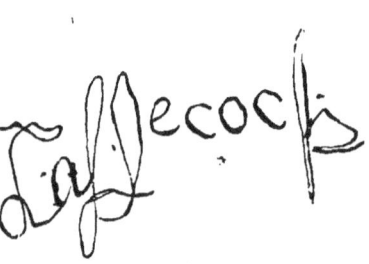

July 29, 1735. Several Indians of Conestogoe and Susquehannah, to the number of Thirty in all, Men, Women & Children, coming to town on a friendly visit, a council was held.

COUNCIL AT PHILADIA., August 1st, 1735. Thomas Penn, Esqr. Proprietary.

Civility, by the Interpreter, said:

That there are now present three different Nations of the Indians, to witt: the Conestogoes, Ganawese, and Shawanese, who are come down to visit the Proprietors, and to renew with them the League & Chain of Friendship.

These Indians at a Council held at Philadia., August 2, 1735, ratified the second and last Great Treaty of Amity.

THE TREATY.—Articles of Agreement Indented, Made, Concluded, & Agreed upon at Philadelphia, the twenty-third day of the second Month called April, in the year One thousand seven hundred and one, between William Penn,[1] Proprietary and Governor of the Province of Pennsylvania and Territories thereunto belonging, on the one Part, And Connoodaghtoh, King of the Indians inhabiting upon and about the River Susquehannah in the said Province, And

The second great treaty between the Founder and the Indians.

[1] It was the Founder's intention to locate a second Philadelphia on the Susquehanna. "And I do also intend that every one who shall be a purchaser in the proposed Settlement shall have a proportionable lot in the Said City to build a house or houses upon, which town ground and the shares of land that shall be bought by me shall be delivered clear of all Indian pretentions, for it has been my way from the first to purchase their title from them and so settle with their consent." Proposals of William Penn, 1690.—*Hazard's Rep.*, Vol. I., p. 400.

Widgh (alias Orytyagh), Koqueash and Andaggy-junkquagh, Chiefs of the said Nations of Indians,[1] And Wopaththa King, & Lenroytungh, & Penroyajooag!! Chiefs of the Nations of the Shawonnah Indians, And Ahookassoongh, Brother to the Emperor, for & in Behalf of the Emperor (& Weewhinjough, Cheequittagh Takyewsan & Woapatkoa, Chiefs), of the Nations of the Indians inhabiting in & about the Northern part of the River Potomock, in the said Province, for and in Behalf of, themselves and successors, and their several Nations and People, on the other part, as followeth :

That as hitherto there hath always been a Good Understanding & Neighbourhood between the said William Penn and his Lieutenant since his first Arrival in the said Province, and the several Nations of Indians inhabiting in & about the same, so there shall be for ever hereafter, a firm and everlasting Peace continued between the said William Penn, his Heirs and Successors, & all the English and other Christian Inhabitants of the said Province, & the said Kings & Chiefs & their Successors, & all the several People of the Nations of Indians aforesaid, and that they shall for ever hereafter be as one As one head and one heart together. head & one heart, & live in true Friendship and Amity as one People. Item, that the said Kings and Chiefs (each for himself & his People En-

---

[1] The Conestogas were the remains of a tribe of the six nations settled at Conestogoe, and thence called Conestogoe Indians. On the first arrival of the English

gaging) shall at no time hurt, injure or Defraud, or suffer to be hurt, Injured or Defrauded, by any of their Indians, an Inhabitant or Inhabitants of the said Province, either in their Persons or Estates. And that the said William Penn, his heirs and successors, shall not suffer to be Done or Committed by any of the Subjects of England within the said Province, any act of Hostilities. or Violence, Wrong or Injury to or against any of the said Indians, but shall on both sides at all times readily do Justice & perform all Acts and Offices of Friendship & Good Will, to oblige Each other to a lasting Peace as. aforesaid. Item that all & every the said Kings and Chiefs & all & every particular of the Nations under them, shall at all times behave themselves Regularly and Soberly, according to the Laws of this Government, while they live near or amongst the Christian Inhabitants. thereof. And that the said Indians shall have the full & free privileges & Immunities of all the said Laws as. any other Inhabitants, they duly Owning and Acknowledgg. the Authority of the Crown of England and

in Pennsylvania, messengers from this tribe came to welcome them with presents of venison, corn and skins, and the whole tribe entered into a treaty of friendship with the first proprietor, William Penn, which was to last as long as the sun should shine or the water run in the rivers. This treaty has been since frequently renewed and the chain brightened, as they expressed, from time to time. It has never been violated on their part or ours till now. A narrative, etc., printed in the year MDCCLXIV. (written and printed by Benjamin Franklin).—*Hist. Soc. Lib.*

Of these Indians, in the year 1764, but twenty remained, of these one Shehaw was a very old man, having assisted at the second treaty held with them by William, Penn in 1701.—*Ib.* [4.]

Government of this Province. Item, that none of the said Indians shall at any time be Aiding, Assisting, or Abetting to any other Nation, whether of Indians or others that shall not at such time be in Amity with the said Crown of England & of this Government. Item, that if at any time any of the Indians, by means of Evil minded Persons & Sowers of Sedition should hear any unkind or Disadvantageous Reports of the English as if they had Evil Designs agst. any of the said Indians, in such case such Indians shall send notice thereof to the said William Penn, his heirs or successors, or their Lieutenants, and shall not give Credence to the said Reports, till by that means they shall be fully satisfied concerning the Truth thereof, and that the said William Penn, his heirs and successors or their Lieutenants shall at all times in such cases do the Like by them. Item, that the said Kings & Chiefs & their successors & People, shall not suffer any strange Nation of Indians to settle or plant on the further side of Susquehannah, or about Potomock River, but such as are there already seated, nor bring any other Indians into any part of this Province, without the special Approbation & Permission of the said William Penn, his heirs & successors.

Item, That for the prevention of Abuses that are too frequently put upon the said Indians in trade ; that the said William Penn, his heirs & Successors, shall not suffer or permit any Person to trade or commerce with any of the said Indians, but such as shall be first allowed or approved of by an Instrument under the hand & seal of him, the said William Penn, or his heirs, or Successors, or their Lieutenants, and, that the said Indians shall suffer no Person whatsoever to buy or sell or have commerce with any of them the said Indians, but such as shall first be approved as aforesaid.

Item, that the said Indians shall not Sell or Dispose of any of their Skins, Peltry or Furs, or any other Effects of their hunting, to any Person or Persons whatsoever out of the Province, nor to any other Person but such as shall be authorized to trade with them as aforesaid, and that for their Encouragement the said William Penn, his heirs & Successors, shall take care to have them the said Indians, duly furnished with all sorts of necessary goods for their use at Reasonable Rates.

Item, that the Potomock Indians aforesaid, with their Colony, shall have free leave of the said William Penn, to settle upon any part of Potomock River within the Bounds of this Province, they strictly observing & practising all & singular the Articles aforesaid, to them relating.

Item, the Indians of Conestogoe and upon and about the River Susquehannah, and more especially the said Connoodaghtah their King, doth fully agree to, and by these presents absolutely Ratifie the Bargain & Sale of Land lying near & about the said River formerly made to the said William Penn, his heirs & Successors, and since by Orytyagh & Andaggy-junkquagh, parties to these presents confirmed to the said William Penn, his heirs & Successors, by a Deed bearing date the thirteenth day of September last, under their hands & Seals, duly Executed; and the said Connoodaghtah doth for himself and his Nation, covenant and agree that he will at all times be ready further to confirm and make good the said Sale according to the Tenour of the same, and that the said Indians of Susquehannah shall answer to the said William Penn, his heirs & Successors, for the good Behaviour and Conduct of the said Potomock Indians, and for their performance of the several Articles herein expressed.

Item, the said William Penn doth hereby promise for himself, his heirs & Successors, that he and they will at _{True friends and brothers.} all times show themselves true Friends and Brothers, to all & every of the said Indians, by assisting them with the best of their Advices, Directions, & Councils, and will in all things Just and Reasonable Befriend them, they behaving themselves as aforesaid, and submitting to the Laws of this Province in all things as the English and other Christians therein Doe, to which they the said Indians hereby agree and obliedge themselves and their Posterity for ever. In Witnesse whereof the said Parties have, as a Confirmation, made mutual Presents to each other; the Indians in five Parcells of Skins, and the said William Penn in several English Goods and Merchandize, as a binding pledge of the premises, never to be Broken or Violated, and as a further Testimony thereof, have also to these presents Interchangeably sett their hands and seals the Day and Year above written:

Connoodaghtah,	[L. S.]	Wopaththa,	[L. S.]
Andaggy-junkquagh,	[L. S.]	Ahookassoough,	[L. S.]
Penroyajooagh,	[L. S.]	Takyewsan,	[L. S.]
Cheequittagh,	[L. S.]	Koqueeash,	[L. S.]
Widaagh,		Lernoytung,	[L. S.]
als.		Weewhinjough,	[L. S.]
Orytyagh	[L. S.]	Woapatkoa,	[L S.]

Signed, Sealed & Delivered In the presence of
Edward Shippen,   John Sanders,
Nathan Stanbury,
Alaxander Paxton,   Penroquenichchan, his ✗ mark
Caleb Pusey,
James Streater,
J. Le Tort,   Passaquessay, his ✗ mark
Jut Hans Stellman,
James Logan,
Indian Harry, alias Showydoohungh, Interpreter, his ✗ mark

On the occasion of the ratification of this treaty in 1735 Thomas Penn said: And you also see that the great Treaty of Friendship then made, was not for three Generations only but forever, that is as long as the Sun & Moon shall endure, or Water to flow in the Rivers which is the Language that has always been used on these Occasions. And as you now see this, and have one of the Writings in your own hands, you should always, in some Number of years, get some honest English Man to read that Paper to you, that the Contents of it may be kept in Remembrance.

<small>This writing also preserved by the Indians.</small>

These Articles you see were made principally with the Susquehannah Indians, who then mostly lived at Conestogoe: And the Shawanese, as their friends, came also, under our Father's Protection, and entered into the same League. It were to be wished that their whole Nation were made sensible of this, and those of that Nation who were now here are desired very carefully to acquaint the rest with what they have seen & heard here.

And now on these heads there remains no more, that we should here most solemnly Ratify & Confirm all these Articles so far as they relate to Friendship and Union, to be observed not only by us but our Posterity to all Generations.

<small>And now on these heads there remains no more.</small>

At the conclusion of this Council the governor presented a large belt of Wampum.—*Col. Rec.*, Vol. III., pages 654–5.

The following presents were brought by the Indians:

107	Fall Deer skins	at	1–9	each £	9.7.3
21	Ordinary	"	1	"	1.1.0
35	Indian Drest	"	3–6	"	6.2.6
4	Raccoons	"	1–6	"	0.6.0
2	Bear skins	"	4	"	0.8.0
					17.4.9

And the following goods valued at £30 were procured for and presented to them:

4 fine guns	20 pounds powder
8 Shawls	40 pounds lead
8 Blankets	30 Knives
8 Shirts	50 Flints
4 Hats	

with some rum, pipes, tobacco, and bread, which the Indians received with great thankfulness, together with the charges of their entertainment provided by the Proprietary's treasurer.

With this we close the citations confirmatory of the first treaty with the Indians—the establishment of a lasting confidence and unity of interest which was a chief object of his coming; and to which the land purchases were subsidiary.

These citations from letters, councils, proclamations, and other writings establish the fact that there was executed by the Founder at his first coming in 1682 a great Treaty of Amity with the Indian tribes; and that at his second coming in pursuance of the same purpose he entered into a second great Treaty of Amity.

That both treaties were committed to writing in a formal manner; that the chief heads of the first treaty and the whole body of the writing of the second are still extant in our colonial records, and that these treaties were renewed from time to time by his sons and governors.

The policy then inaugurated has never been departed from by our State.

Through that policy the hand of violence against the Indian has been stayed, and the chain brightened and kept clean and without rust even to these years.

It is therefore that the Founder has received homage from men of all opinions—and that that first treaty—renewed and confirmed by himself, his sons and his governors from year to year and made part of the very structure of our State, still survives, and will forever live in the world's common memory.

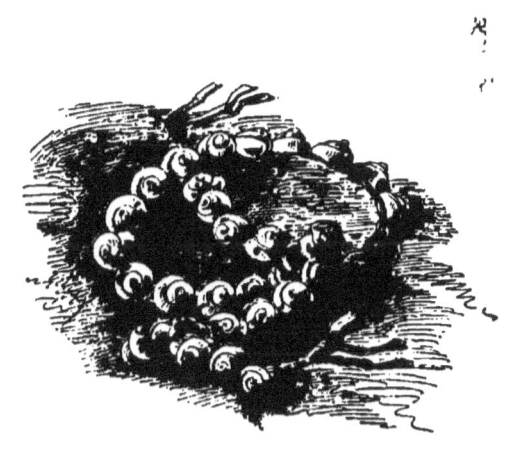

THE TRADITION AMONG THE INDIANS.

BETWEEN the years 1770 and 1780, they could relate very minutely what had passed between William Penn and their forefathers, at their first meeting and afterwards, and also the transactions

which took place with the governors who succeeded him.—*Heckewelder*, p. 107.

In the year 1781 there were still some very aged Indians living on the banks of the Muskingum who were present when the first houses were built in Philadelphia. They related that the white people treated them with the greatest kindness, so that they appeared to be but one nation.—*Loskiel La Trobe*, p. 1., Ch. X., p. 124.

Thus we find that the lapse of one hundred years had

not obliterated in the minds of the Indians the tender feelings which the kindness and upright conduct of their brother Mignon (so the Delawares called William Penn) had inspired, and, no doubt, in the dreary solitudes beyond the Mississippi, to which their miserable remnants have been driven by a policy to which history will give its true name, those poor exiles from the land of their ancestors still teach their children to lisp the name of

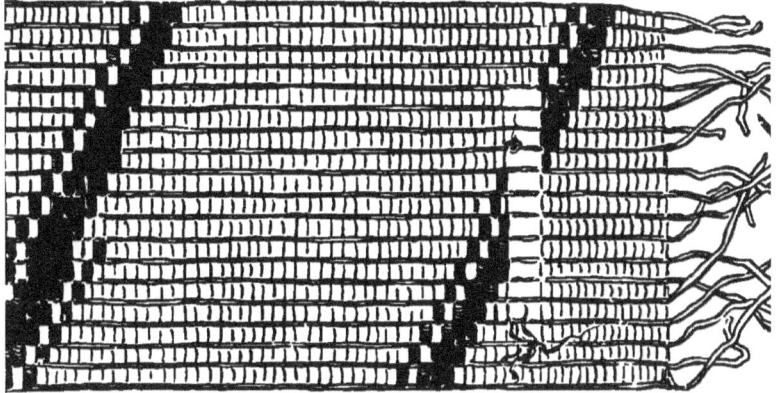

their friend Mignon, with far different feelings from those with which they refer to names of more modern date.—*H. M. S. of Pa.*, Vol. III., P. II., p. 148.

And still he has not forgotten the great treaty, and among the scattered remnants of those once powerful tribes, now seated by the clear lakes of Canada or wandering on the banks of the turbid Missouri, the name of the great and the good Onas continues to be held in grateful remembrance.—*Janney*, p. 209.

THE STATEMENTS OF THE WRITERS AS TO THE TREATY ARE AS FOLLOWS

OLDMIXON.—"The British Empire in America," was written about twenty-five years after the first arrival of William Penn in this country. In it he states that "the proprietary, upon his arrival in his Colony, entered into treaties with the Indians to buy lands." Afterwards, however, speaking of Penn's removal to England, in 1684, he particularly mentions the treaties of friendship that he made with the Aborigines. Mr. Penn, he says, stayed in Pennsylvania two years, and having made a league of amity with nineteen Indian nations, between them and all the English in America; having established good laws, he returned to England. —*Oldmixon*, 1708, London, p. 171.

PROUD.—Mr. Proud's history of Pennsylvania was published in the year 1797. In it he mentions the purchases of land by William Penn, but after having spoken of these, he writes: "It was at this time (1682) when he (William Penn) first entered personally into that lasting friendship with the Indians, which ever after continued between them.

"Again he says a firm peace was thereupon concluded

between William Penn and the Indians, and both parties mutually promised to live together as brethren, without doing the least injury to each other. This treaty was solemnly ratified by the mutual token of a chain of friendship, a covenant indelible, never to be broken as long as the sun and moon endure."—*Proud's History*, Vol. I., p. 212.

GORDON finally writes in his history it has been doubted whether the conference between William Penn and the Indians was holden under the great Elm at Shackamaxon, and whether it was accompanied by a formal treaty. If we suffer ourselves to doubt these facts, historical tradition is unworthy of acceptance, and little credence can be given to ordinary historical testimony.—*Gordon's Pennsylvania*, p. 603.

RAYNAL.—The Abbe Raynal, in his Continent embracing work, wrote: "He (William Penn) signalized his arrival by an act of equity by which he endeared his person and made his principles acceptable."—*Raynal's Hist. Philos.*

VOLTAIRE.—Voltaire, who was without faith in anything human or divine save Pennsylvania and the purposes of its founder, gave in his credence by the yet more often quoted passage:

"The only treaty which has not been sworn to, and which has not been broken." It appears in every notice of the Founder's life. The whole passage reads: " He began by making a league with the American Indians

which were his neighbors. This is the only treaty between those persons and the Christians which has not been sworn to, and which has not been broken."
"C'est le seul traite entre ces peuples et les Chretiens qui n'ait point ete jure et qui n'ait point ete rompu."—*Dict. Philos.*, 7, 17-18.

ARMISTEAD, who drew from original sources, repeats the story. "In 1682 Penn first entered into that lasting friendship with the Indians which ever afterwards continued between them."—*Armistead's Life of James Logan*, p. 85.

The fact that a treaty at his first coming was made, was committed to writing kept for many years, and cited again and again by its heads, having been established by these records with the concurrence of all who have written upon it, without any exception; there only remains the question of the place, the season, and the year in which it was held, and the attending circumstances; these rest on tradition, but tradition of the most reliable character, both in certainty of statement and the persons by whom it was made.

This is fortified by its acceptance by historians of the highest reliability, and by the patient researches of the Historical Society of the State, where it was alleged to have taken place, on two occasions, in which all that then existed was examined, and the conclusion reached to which this writer has also come.

THE PLACE OF THE TREATY.—But it is almost indisputably probable, said the venerable Judge Peters, if general tradition did not confirm the fact, that William Penn chose to hold this treaty beyond the reach of any jealousy about the neighborhood of fortified places and within the lines of his province far from such places; and at a spot (Shackamaxon) which had been an Indian settlement familiar to and esteemed by the natives, and where neither Dutch nor Swedes could be supposed to have influence, for with them the Indians had bickerings. This view of the subject gives the strongest confirmation to the tradition of the Treaty being held at Kensington.[1]

Shackamaxon was a place of resort for the Indians of different Nations, no doubt to consult together and settle their mutual concerns, and while it comes in aid of our etymology of that name, it accounts for its having been chosen by Markham and William Penn after him, as the place for holding their successive treaties. It adds also no little importance to the locality of the great treaty under the Elm Tree.[2]

The tradition rests on the following direct testimony, says Judge Peters. I have always understood and believed that the treaty in 1682 was held at Shackamaxon. When a boy I have resorted to the great Elm Tree, and have always confided in the then uncontradicted tradition that under that tree the treaty was held. The place had been an Indian Village 57 years ago.

[1] Richard Peters to Roberts Vaux, Belmont, Sep. 6, 1825.
[2] *Mem. H. S. of Pa.*, Vol. III., p. 2, p. 184.

Both David Conyngham and myself remember when boys, bathing on the sandy beach near the famous Elm. No person then disputed the fact that this Elm was the tree under which Penn's treaty was held. Mr. Conyngham remembers distinctly, the friendly visitation of Benjamin Lay to the scene of our sports. He must have been known to some of the contemporaries of Penn. After dilating on the worth and virtues of that good man, and particularly as they applied to the treatment of the natives, he would call on the boys; point out the Elm Tree and enjoin on them to bear in mind, and teach to their children that under that tree Penn's treaty was held and they should respect it accordingly.

Strength is added to this by the general acceptance of the tradition, so that during the revolutionary war the British General Simcoe, who was quartered at Kensington so regarded it that whilst his soldiers were felling the trees of the vicinity for fuel, he placed a sentinel under this tree that not a branch of it might be touched. Statement by General Simcoe to Sir B. West.—*Memoirs of H. S. of Pa.*, 1825, p. 97.

That this treaty, therefore, says the Society, was held at Shackamaxon shortly after the arrival of William Penn in 1682 we think that the least doubt cannot at present be entertained.[2]

[1] Richard Peters, Belmont, November 3, 1825.
[2] *H. S. of Pa.*, Vol. VI., p. 94.

THE SEASON OF THE YEAR.—As to this the Society says:
We consider ourselves at liberty to fix the epoch of
the great treaty at such time as we shall think most consistent with probability, and we believe that to be about
the latter end of November. The season was then
beautiful, as is generally the fall season in our country.
His journey lasted about a month, and he had sufficient
time to go to New York and Long Island, visit his
friends on the way in Pennsylvania and New Jersey,
and treat with the Indians on his return. On his departure from New Castle, his friend Markham had full
time to give notice to the Chiefs to meet him at Shackamaxon; in short, by adopting this period we find ourselves free from the objections that meet us at every
step in choosing any other.[1]

THE SPEECHES ON THE OCCASION.—As to these the
Society further says: What he (Clarkson) relates of the
speech of William Penn, appears to us conformable to
the best traditions, and to agree in substance, with the
information that we have been able to collect elsewhere,
from various sources. It was natural that he should explain to the Indians the principles of the Society of
Friends on the subject of bearing arms, and we may well
suppose that he began his speech as Mr. Clarkson relates.
Also that he should tell them that the land which they
had sold, or should sell to the Whites, was to be held in
common between them, and that both nations should be

[1] *Mem. H. S. of Pa.*, Vol. III., p. 2, 150, 185.

at liberty to occupy it for their lawful purposes. It is entirely in accordance with what we have said of the opinions of the Indians respecting property; and that this language was held by the proprietor, is fully ascertained by the speeches of the Governor of the Colony and those of the Indians in subsequent treaties.—*Mem. H. S. of Pa.*, Vol. III., P. II., p. 166-189. *Clarkson's Life.*

The tradition does not rest upon the words or writings of inconsiderate men, it has come down to us from the lips of men, one with whom falsehood was impossible, another taught by a life of judicial training to disbelieve except upon the clearest evidence, another incredulous from his nature, another exhaustive in researches, another the friend and companion of the Founder; with these that body of men who devote their lives to these investigations, and who lived as it were on the very ground.

THE CONSERVATORS of the tradition

James Logan was born in Ireland in 1674 or '75, embarked with Penn for Pennsylvania 7th mo. (Sep.), 1699. Arrived 10th mo. (Dec.); when Penn returned to England 3rd, 9ber., 1701, he then 25, was made Secretary of the Province by Penn, and had general charge of the Government and property. "I have left thee," wrote Penn, "in an uncommon trust with a singular dependence on thy justice and care." He discharged his duties with fidelity and friendship; he was long Chief Justice of the Province and held the Office of Commissioner of Property. He was two years President of the Council and ex-officio Governor of the Province. In 1738 he retired from the Presidency. The Indians visited and sometimes remained under his hospitality until his death. At a treaty held with the Six Nations at Philadelphia, July, 1742, which he could not attend by reason of a bodily infirmity, they brought him a present of a bundle of skins, and Conasatego, Chief of the Onondagoes speaking for the chiefs, said of him to Governor Thomas: "James Logan is a wise man and a fast friend of the Indians, and we desire when his soul goes to God you may choose in his room just such another person." He died 31st, 10 mo., 1751, aet. 77. The Loganian Library then his private library the collection of 50 years was his bequest to the City of Philadelphia.—*Armistead's Logan*, passim, and p. 86. *Hugh's Penn*, p. 91.

BENJAMIN LAY was born in England in 1677; as a sailor he voyaged to Syria; there he sought out where the Saviour conversed with the woman of Samaria, and refreshed him with water from Jacob's Well. He was one of those men who come into the world exciting consternation and disquiet. In 1718 he was in business in Barbadoes, where the horrors of slavery and the hatred of the owners of the slaves forced him to leave. He came to Philadelphia in 1731. His form and features were very ungainly, but his countenance lighted with a lofty and calm benignity: in his new home he fought alone his solitary idea. His kindly heart finally breaking down into misanthropy, he made himself a cave near the city, weaving his own clothes and living on the fruits of his orchard. He would eat no flesh, and nothing that came from the labor of slaves. So qualified he went forth to preach his doctrine. In 1737 he wrote his book, "All Slavekeepers that keep the innocent in bondage, apostates." Richard Penn and Franklin visited him in his cave, the latter corresponded with him through his life: he wrote also for prisoners and visited the children in the schools. From his cave hung down evergreens: it contained a library of 200 volumes. His hatred of money accumulation was extreme. These lines were written on the blank leaves of one of his books found after the war:

"O, the blessed doctrine and practice of the first Christians which kept out luxury, pride, and cursed covetousness." He died on 3rd, 2nd Mo. (Feb.) 1759, anno aetatis 82. He lived twenty-eight years of his life in Pennsylvania.—*Vaux's Life* (1815).

BENJAMIN WEST was born at Springfield, Chester county, in Pennsylvania, October 10, 1738. His father was an English Quaker who came over with Penn on his second voyage in 1699. He was taught to mix colors by a party of Indians who visited his father's house. At nine years he was painting portraits of real worth, and which, in his estimation, were in some features of handling never surpassed by him. He was brought to Philadelphia and studied classical literature under Dr. Smith, of the University of Pennsylvania. His reputation finally reached over all Europe and America. The treaty was an early production, in the opinion of John Sartain, rendered certain by his mode of laying on the color which was abandoned in his later years. There existed an early picture of the Treaty by him which the family prized very highly but which was lost. He therefore a second time and on a large canvass determined to perpetuate his credence in the tradition.[1] No one of all the authorities was situated as favorably as himself to know the verity of the tradition. His family, fellow-voyagers of the Founder, Quakers and residents of an adjoining county; his first instructors, the Indians themselves; his own residence in his early years in Philadelphia, his associations English; and his second picture painted for, or coming into the possession of the Founder's family. With this, his entire credibility. He was unmoved by the applause of the world or the

[1] Hall's engraving of the second picture, now in the Museum, Philadelphia, the gift of the late Joseph Harrison's family, was made prior to 1775.—*Encyc. West Edinb. Encyc. West.*

A letter to the Rev. William Smith, Stoke, May 30, 1775, by Juliana Penn, wife of the Governor, John Penn, states:

"I can send nothing from here but which some friend will take privately, which prevents me sending at the same time a print from a painting of Mr. West's on the subject of the settlement of your province, but shall take the first opportunity to send you one of them likewise."—*Rev. William Smith's Life and Correspondence*, Vol. I., p. 503.

Mr. Clarkson, who wrote the biography of William Penn, in 1813, told J. Francis Fisher, of Philadelphia, that he was indebted for his information on the subject of this Treaty to our celebrated painter, Benjamin West.—*Hist. Trans. A. P. S.* 176.

smiles of the great, and there was not in all his life a spot or blemish on his character. He died March, 1820, and was buried in St. Paul's, London.

JOHN OLDMIXON was born in 1673; of him Macaulay says, what certainly applies to that writer in equal measure, "His assertions unsupported by evidence are of no weight whatever." "The British Empire" was published in 1708. The writer was contemporaneous with the Founder, and his assertions as to the Treaty were very probably supported by the Founder: much of his information he alleges came from Penn himself, and, unlike the assertions of the other, is supported by the Founder's whole life and character.

RICHARD PETERS was born at Belmont, now in the Park of Philadelphia, in 1744. He was the nephew of Richard Peters who was Secretary of the land office in the years 1737 to 1747. He filled the office of Secretary of the Board of War during the Revolution; was a representative in Congress, and was a Judge of the United States District Court thirty-nine years. He died August 22, 1828, aet. 84.

SAMUEL BRECK was born in Boston, July 17, 1771; lived at Sweet Briar, now in the Park of Philadelphia, thirty-eight years. He was four years a State Senator, where he made his name memorable by his bill for the final emancipation of the slaves in Pennsylvania. He was a member of the 18th Congress, and again served in the State Senate, when he drew the bill to establish

the Common School System of Pennsylvania. He was
one of the founders of the Institution for the Blind in
Philadelphia; he lived through every event in the foun
dation of our National Government from the first battle
for our independence, which he witnessed, a child in his
nurse's arms, and through the first seventy battles of the
war for the emancipation of the slaves. His last words
were: "What of my Country?" He died August 22,
1862.

The writers also remain accredited and standard to
this day.

ROBERT PROUD was born May 10, 1728; he was closely
associated with the Friends as a teacher of their children: his work was commenced in 1791; its merit is in
the value and reliability of its material, and the honesty
of the chronicler. He came from England and got to
Philadelphia January 6, 1759. He died 7th of July,
1813, aged eighty-six years. He was a quaint but reliable relic of the old rule, wearing a curled gray wig,
cocked patriarchal hat, and long ivory-headed cane; he
was in person tall, with a great Roman nose extending
out from under a most impending brow. He began his
work in 1791, when the remembrance of the story of the
event was still fresh in the minds of the living generation who had heard it from their fathers.

THE ABBE RAYNAL'S Histoire Philosophique et politique appeared in 1770 in 4 volumes; it was reprinted
in 20 successive editions to 1820, when it appeared in

Yours, truly
Thomas Clarkson

the Paris edition of 12 volumes. It has been translated into all the languages of modern literature, assailed, approved, condemned, criticized, annotated, illustrated in almost every mode possible to literature, yet I can find, in no accessible volume of these, in our own libraries any attack on the credibility of his statement relating to the treaty; in his estimation it stands the sole relief in modern civilization's black horrors of crimes; yet its credibility remains unassailed by the regiments of volumes of criticism against every other part of his work, speaking all the languages of modern times.

GUILLAUME THOMAS RAYNAL was born in 1711, and died March 6th, 1796; the generation following the founder.

THOMAS CLARKSON, the Biographer of the Founder, was one of that despised band of men who a hundred years later trod in the footsteps of his pacific intentions to the human race; and like the Founder was a man of great determination and ceaseless endeavor. His life consumed itself in one object; his first writings and his last were for the deliverance of the negro slaves. In 1785 he took the first prize among the senior bachelors of the University of Cambridge as a Latin essayist; his subject was An ne liceat invitos in servitute dare (Is it right to make Men slaves against their will[1]). He

[1] In the preface to the English translation of his first essay he refers to Las Casas as the first of those who humanely exerted themselves to abolish Indian slavery in the Western colonies, and says this amiable man was so sensibly affected at the treatment which the miserable Indians underwent, that he made a remonstrance before the celebrated Emperor Charles the V., declaring that heaven would one day call him to account for those cruelties. An Essay by T. Clarkson, Phila., 1810, p. iii–vii.

wrote continuously on this single theme, first a translation of this essay & other essays in 1783-87-89-91-1807, and other indefatigable work until slavery was abolished in the British Empire. He then sought to make the objects of the Founder, of which this was one, & which he understood & lived so thoroughly, as well understood by others; he wrote for this purpose his portraiture of quakerism in 1809; and he crowned his literary career with "The public and private life of William Penn," in 1813; it is in this work he wrote the description of "The Treaty" which is made almost impregnable by the documents cited in this Volume. It is most evident that there must have existed at some time in the West or other quaker family of Pennsylvania a written account of the treaty and the speeches on the occasion; the verification of the incidents and language as given to Clarkson being so exactly maintained by the documents now in our possession but inaccessible to either West or himself; except the reference to the laying the parchment on the ground which did occur later in the purchase of the Conestogoes' title and probably also the casting down their arms, there is everything confirmatory of the action and even the language used. In the memoirs of William Penn he spared no pains nor labor to inform himself of every circumstance relative to Penn, whether contained in well known or obscure works (*Lond. Eclec. Review*). He performed his undertaking with the zeal of an affectionate admirer and with taste, judgment and accuracy (*London Chris. Adv.*) Few men of far reaching intentions have attained the goal for which they set out in their lives; it was otherwise with this good as well as illustrious man; he lived to see the heavily burthened, overtaxed people of England in the most honourable manner, and in the most strict conformity with the founder's example purchase the slaves of the British colonies at a fair valuation—a title of a more baseless character than that of the aborigines, and which this Country considered of as little value and finally settled in the same manner as they had done the English titles themselves.

He was born on the 28th March, 1760, and died in 1846, aged 86 years.

TO this weight of testimony the only answer has been the silence about the treaty at the time, and this equally applies to all the leagues of amity then and thereafter made, but to this the answer with which we conclude; what most distinguishes such characters as the founder, in the eyes of posterity, seems the least worthy of record to them in their lives or in the opinion of their contemporaries. Sales of lands, exchanges of trade and other matters having present interest, and use, create their certain records everywhere; events that change the destinies of after ages, are without present value, and gain them real importance only in the later ages when the results of these events, eventuate. Sentiments do not get into the statutes of legislatures, unless they are written at the time with a sword.

It is therefore that they endure the longer; the records of trade perish with its merchandise; the work of the sword rusts away with the sword; these wiser, kindlier purposes survive the grave itself, which consumes all else.

This tradition is as the tree was with which it is associated; time which gave it strength and value was powerless to change its form and character, or excise its beginning from the place where it took root in the credence of our forefathers; its existence there, in their lives, was the unanswerable argument of its past existence there, and the concentric rings within its core did not count backward more certainly, than the tradition itself does, to the very year when the bounteous shoot from which it grew to be the glory of our State, was set there by the pious hand of our founder.

THE TREATY TREE.

> "Tho' time has devoted our tree to decay,
> The sage lessons it witness'd survive to our day.
> May our trustworthy statesmen when called to the helm,
> Ne'er forget the wise treaty held under our Elm."—RICHARD PETERS.

IT fell during a storm on the night of the 5th of March, 1810. "After a blow from the northeast on Monday last (5th) about 11 o'clock at night the wind shifted to the west and blew a tremendous gale the whole night. A great number of trees in and about the city were blown up by the roots as was also the large tree at Kensington, under which William Penn, the founder of Pennsylvania, signed his first treaty with the Aborigines. This noted tree having stood the blasts of a hundred or more winters since that event, has at last crumbled to the dust. 'True American,' copied into the Register, March 7th, 1810 (Wednesday). After the tree was uprooted it measured 24 feet in circumference."[1]

"The circles of annual growth which its trunk exhibited, then indicated an age of two hundred and eighty-three years."[2]

[1] *H. S. of Pa.*, Vol. I., p. 96.
[2] *Ibid.*, Vol. I., p. 240.

"Samuel Breck visited it as it lay in ruins, and took from it a limb, which he gave to Captain Watson, of the British Navy, to deposit it in the Museum of Exeter, in England."[1]

After its fall in a more unpoetical, but more substantial manner than the ashes of Wickliffe, it passed away from the Delaware to the ocean, and has been distributed in canes, boxes, desks and all manner of other forms to other countries.

On the occasion of Lafayette's visit (1824-5) John F. Watson presented him with a box composed of pieces of wood among which was a piece of the Treaty Elm; "a branch of the old tree was then growing in the garden of the hospital under which our fellow-citizens delighted to recount the story of its origin while protected by its shade."[2] One stood in the centre of Clinton street near Ninth, in Mr. Armstrong's memory. A large piece was sent to John Penn of Stoke Park, England, on which he had inscribed: "A remnant of the great Elm Tree under which the treaty was held between William Penn and the Indians soon after his landing in America, in 1682, and which grew at Kensington, near Philadelphia, till the autumn of the year 1810, when it fell during a storm: was presented to his grandson, John Penn."[3]

[1] Samuel Breck, *Mem. H. S. of Pa.*, Vol. VI., p. 213.
[2] *Levasseur's Lafayette*, Vol. II., p. 232.
[3] *Hugh's Penn*, p. 95.

Dr. Rush had an arm-chair made from the wood of the then far-famed Elm Tree, and sent an ink-stand made of it to Dr. Roscoe, of Liverpool.[1]

On receiving from Dr. Rush, this piece of the tree under which William Penn made his Treaty with the Indians, he wrote the following lines:

> "From clime to clime, from shore to shore,
> The War fiend raised his horrid yell,
> And midst the storm which realms deplore,
> Penn's honored tree of Concord fell.
>
> "And of that tree that ne'er again
> Shall Spring's reviving influence know,
> A relic o'er the Atlantic main
> Was sent, the gift of foe to foe.[2]
>
> "But though no more its ample shades
> Wave green beneath Columbia's sky,
> Though every branch be now decayed,
> And all its scattered leaves be dry,
>
> "Yet midst the relic's sainted space,
> A health-restoring flood shall spring,
> In which the angel form of peace
> May stoop to dip her dove-like wing.
>
> "So once that staff the prophet bore,
> By wondering eyes again was seen
> To swell with life through every pore,
> And bud afresh with foliage green.
>
> "The withered branch again shall grow,
> Till o'er the earth its shade extend;
> And this, the gift of foe to foe,
> Becomes the gift of friend to friend.

[1] *Wakefield's Penn.* Preface.
[2] Alluding to the state of hostilities between the two countries (1812).

At the Anniversary of the Landing in 1824, two armchairs made of the wood of the Elm Tree under which William Penn held his Treaty with the Indians in 1682 were presented by John F. Watson.

The centre of the table was ornamented with a model of the monument made by Haviland, of part of the treaty tree.[1]

Thomas Birch, the marine painter, by whom the drawing of the treaty tree in this volume was made in 1801, was the son of William Birch, who published the print; he told John Sartain that he might rely on it that he drew the tree for his father and that every branch and twig as he saw it there, was delineated by him in this drawing.[2] His son, the present Thomas Birch, of Philadelphia, said that he told him he had bestowed on the drawing that same care that he would have done on a portrait, that every branch and twig was delineated by him.[3] Mr. Birch has also preserved a frame made of the wood of the old tree presented by Mr. Franklin Eyre, its last owner.

In 1848 "the County Commissioners of Philadelphia County were vested with power and authority to purchase and hold for public use the lot or piece of ground described as the site of Penn's Treaty with the Indians as authorized and requested by the Philadelphia County Board in the year 1848, the cost not to exceed the amount appropriated by the said County Board for the purchase thereof.[4]

[1] Proceedings of the meeting. Franklin Inst. Library.
[2] Relation of John Sartain to the author, 1882.
[3] Relation of Thomas Birch to the author, 1882.
[4] Ap. 9, 1849. *Laws of Pa.*, 1849, p. 540.

In 1827 the Penn Society erected a monument there. It bears the following inscription:

Treaty Ground	Pennsylvania
of	founded
William Penn	1681
and the	By Deeds of Peace.
Indian Nations	
1682	Raised by the
Unbroken Faith.	Penn Society
	A. D. 1827
William Penn	to mark the
Born 1644.	site of the
Died 1718.	Great Elm Tree.

BRANCH FROM AN ELM NOW GROWING
ON THE TREATY GROUND.

THE FOUNDER'S WORK AND WORTH.

A TESTIMONY OF FRIENDS IN PENNSYLVANIA concerning their deceased friend and Governor, William Penn.

"Yet it becomes us particularly to say, that as he was our Governor, he merited from us love and true honor, and we cannot but have the same regard to his memory, when we consider the blessings and ease we have enjoyed under his government; and are rightly sensible of his care, affection and regard, always shown with anxious concern for the safety and prosperity of the people, who many of them, removed from comfortable livings to be adventurers with him, not so much with views of better acquisitions, or greater riches, but the laudable prospect of retired, quiet habitations for themselves and posterity, and the promotion of truth and virtue in the earth. And as his love was great and endeavors constant for the happiness of his friends, countrymen and fellow-subjects, so was his great tenderness, justice and love towards the Indians, from first to last, always conspicuous and remarkable.

"More might be truly said of him as he was the proprietary and Governor of this Province; and we now find it our duty (incited thereto by the love of our Heavenly Father in our souls), to add a few lines concerning him, as he was our worthy elder, friend and brother in the blessed Truth; many of us having been often comforted, edified and solaced with him in the enjoyment thereof. As was his testimony, so was his conversation, edifyin ; and lovely, administering grace and knowledge. His behaviour was sweet and engaging, and his condescension great, even to the weakest and meanest; affable and of easy access, tender of every person and thing that had simplicity of truth, or honesty for a foundation.

"If William Penn did not accomplish, in the settlement of Pennsylvania, all that his ardent and comprehensive mind originally anticipated, he unquestionably effected more towards establishing the practicability of supporting a government upon strictly Christian principles, than ever was effected by any other man. To disarm by lenient means the wild and untutored inhabitants of the woods; to obtain possession by fair and honorable purchase of such an extensive tract of country, without exciting a murmur amongst its original occupants; to bring so many discordant tribes into treaties of friendship and peace; and to establish an intercourse with them, which was maintained on friendly terms as long as the authorities of Pennsylvania adhered to the principles of the Founder, was certainly to set an important example to succeeding ages. If we judge from the history of the early settlers in New England and Virginia, we shall probably adopt the conclusion that there is quite as much difficulty in maintaining the relations of peace with such people as those who occupied the forests of North America, as with the civilized nations of Europe; yet from the experience of William Penn's settlement here, we have ample reason to believe that if the whole continent of North America had been colonized upon the same Christian principles, and the system been steadily maintained, we might at this day have pointed to the Western world for a verification of the prophetic declaration, that 'nation should not lift up sword against nation, or the people learn war any more.'

"Signed at the time of our general meeting held in Philadelphia, the 16th of the first month, 1718-19."— *Friend's Library*, Vol. V., p. 328.

THE TESTIMONY OF READING MEETING in England, cited by J. Francis Fisher:

"He was a man of great abilities; of an excellent sweetness of disposition; quick of thought and ready of utterance, full of the qualifications of true discipleship, even love without dissimulation; as extensive in charity, as comprehensive in knowledge, and to whom malice and ingratitude were utter strangers; so ready to forgive enemies, that the ungrateful were not excepted.

"In fine, he was learned without vanity; apt without forwardness; facetious in conversation, yet weighty and serious. Of an extraordinary greatness of mind, yet void of the stain of ambition; as free from rigid gravity, as he was clear of unseemly levity; a man, a scholar, a friend, a minister, surpassing in speculative endowments, whose memory will be valued with the wise, and blessed with the just."—*Mem. H. S. of Pa.*, Vol. III., P. II., p. 102.

THE ABBE RAYNAL'S TESTIMONY: "His arrival in the New World was made notable by an Act of Equity, by which he endeared his person and made his principles acceptable. Little satisfied with the right that the cession from the British Ministry had given to his establishment, he determined to purchase from the natives the vast territory he proposed to colonize. He legitimated his possession as much as was in his power; in fine he supplied by the use he made of it, what was wanting in the right of possession. The Americans entertained as much affection for his new colony as they had conceived of estrangement for all those which had been founded in their neighborhood, without consulting their rights or their wishes. Hence a confidence was established between the two peoples, of which nothing could alter the harmony. A mutual good faith bound them more and more closely together.

"The humanity of Penn was not confined to the savages; it extended itself to all those who wished to inhabit his Empire. As the happiness of men depends upon the character of their legislation, he founded his Empire on two principles; the splendor of the State and the happiness of the individual—liberty and property. If it be permitted to use the language of fable for an event which seems fabulous, I would say, that Astraea ascended to heaven since so long a time, had re-descended to earth again, and that the reign of peace and innocence had begun once more among men.

"It is here that the writer and his reader breathe once more; it is here that they find relief from the disgust, the horror and grief which modern history, and especially of the European settlements in America, inspire.

"Until this event possession had meant depopulation; civilization, destruction of the hemisphere, which yet smokes with the blood of its peoples, civilized and savage.

"This virtuous legislator established his Society on the basis of toleration; it was his desire that every man who recognized a Deity, should participate in the rights of citizenship, and every Christian be eligible to State employments. But he left every one at liberty to invoke the Supreme Being as he thought proper. He would not admit a reigning church in Pennsylvania, nor force contributions for building places of public worship, nor compel any person to attend them.

"Penn, attached to his name, was desirous that the propriety of the settlement which he had formed should remain perpetually in his family; but he deprived it of any decisive influence in public resolutions, and ordained that it should not exercise any act of authority without the concurrence of the deputies of the people. Every citizen having an interest in the law by having any in the object of it, was eligible as elector, and might be chosen. To avoid as much as possible every kind of corruption, it was ordained that representatives should be chosen by suffrages secretly given.

"Never perhaps had virtue inspired legislation more conducive to human happiness. Opinions, sentiments and manners corrected what was defective and supplied what was imperfect.

"The prosperity of Pennsylvania was therefore very notable. That Republic without wars, without conquests, without effort, without any of those revolutions which astonish the eyes of the inquiet and passionate, became a spectacle for the entire universe.

" His neighbors, in spite of their barbarity, were enchained by the sweetness of his manners, and strangers, in spite of their corruption, rendered homage to his virtues. Every nation wondered to see realized and renewed the heroic age of antiquity, that the manners and laws of Europe had made seem fabulous."—*Histoire Philosophique. A Geneve,* MDCCLXXX. *Tome Quat.* 272-345. *Merc. Lib.*

NEITHER TO MY FATHER, THE DUKE, NOR THE KING.

THEREFORE, TO THE PEOPLE OF PENNSYLVANIA, THE HAT OF THE FOUNDER, EXPRESSES AUTHORITY MORE ABSOLUTELY THAN ANY DIADEM GLITTERING WITH THE SLAVERY OF THE MINES; SYMBOLIZES FREEDOM MORE ENDURINGLY THAN THE CAP OF THE PHRYGIAN, RED WITH THE REVOLUTIONS OF CENTURIES; ILLUSTRATES CHRISTIANITY MORE TRULY THAN THE MITRE OF WHATEVER PRIESTHOOD, OF WHATEVER THEOLOGY. IT QUIETLY AND PREVAILINGLY ASSERTED, AGAINST PRINCIPALITIES AND POWERS, AND THINGS PRESENT AND THINGS TO COME, THE ULTIMATE EQUALITY, AND DIGNITY OF OUR COMMON HUMANITY.

DAVID McKAY,

SUCCESSOR TO

REES WELSH & CO.'S

MISCELLANEOUS BUSINESS.

Publishers, Booksellers and Importers,

23 SOUTH NINTH STREET,

PHILADELPHIA, PA.

New or Old Books of every description Bought and Sold. Rare old editions of desirable Books a specialty. Orders solicited.

I find, however, that the greatest difficulty lies, not in the selling, but in the procuring of good books, and will esteem it a great favor if any one having a library or any collection of books to dispose of will advise through mail or otherwise.

Above request is made, knowing that I have every facility for using, and therefore can offer terms more satisfactory than houses where books are bought and stored away to await accidental customers.

Very respectfully yours,

DAVID McKAY.

www.ingramcontent.com/pod-product-compliance
Lightning Source LLC
Chambersburg PA
CBHW020138170426
43199CB00010B/802